CAST OF CHARACTERS

The French Leaders

COLETTE MODIANO—the author
M. PARIET—the artistic adviser
CHARLOTTE FLORENT—the Peking University student

The Chinese Leaders

YUAN—who was very much a Party man
SHIN—who wanted to become an engineer, but will become
    a diplomat
SHU—whose trousers looked like a jacket, and her jacket like
    trousers

The Italians

MARQUIS TORTI and SIGNORA COLI—great and good friends
SIGNORA LEANDRI—the stout, deaf, and amiable widow of a
    diplomat
SIGNORA NEGRI—the wife of a Milanese industrialist, and
ISABELLA—her beautiful daughter

The Musketeers

GEORGES WOLF—an art gallery owner
ALEXANDRE DUPONT—a humorous little Swiss
GEORGES NOIRET—a little Napoleon

The Nice Ones

COUNTESS DE CASTILLAT (LAURE)—who was frail and kind
COLETTE QUESNEL—the widow of a newspaper editor
DR. AND MME. BLUM—she spoke excellent Russian
M. AND MME. ADJOUF—he owned much land in Morocco; she
    talked a blue streak
M. AND MME. CHAPEAU—he was in textiles; both were from
    the north of France and were a bit provincial
COUNTESS DE LISSAYE—a handsome socialite
SEÑOR AND SEÑORA NERALINDA—he was a banker; she was a
    maniacal shopper; both were Peruvian

The Inevitable Others

MME. MANDOIS (ADRIENNE)—who was all paint and wigs,
    boots and ski pants
GENERAL DE BOILÈLE—an aristocratic cavalry officer, noisy
    and undiplomatic
MME. TROLLAN—a faded but still haughty beauty; Boilèle's
    companion

CHAIRMAN MAO AND MY MILLIONAIRES

CHAIRMAN MAO AND MY MILLIONAIRES

OR
THROUGH
CHINA
WITH
TWENTY
SNOBS
BY
COLETTE MODIANO

AMERICAN HERITAGE PRESS
A SUBSIDIARY OF McGRAW-HILL
NEW YORK

INTRODUCTION

For the past fifteen years an old friend and I have run a travel agency under the wing of a monthly French art magazine. We organize group tours all over the world, paying the magazine a royalty and in exchange receiving the use of its offices, address, and advertising service. Our freedom has been limited only by the capricious decisions of the editor, the state of the French economy, and the current world political crisis.

In the beginning we were two young people eager to travel at a time when most of the world was still the private preserve of the adventurous and the curious. The magazine has kept us on over the years in two miniscule offices and regarded us with a mixture of astonishment and disbelief, for our enterprise has never failed to show a profit.

My friend and I have traveled the planet enthusiastically, reserving for ourselves the more daring maiden voyages that we did not feel we could entrust to our less experienced colleagues. We have guided groups that have muttered and groups that have rejoiced, but our clients have almost always been satisfied. As a result we have had excellent word-of-mouth publicity among the rich in Western Europe.

My husband, a manufacturer from the French Ardennes, is not always pleased with my frequent trips, but he listens with kindness and interest to the stories I tell on my return. He has even gone so far as to suggest new destinations.

My colleague and I have hardly needed prompting to go farther and farther afield. We have visited Mexico, India, the Middle East, Kenya, Afghanistan, Thailand, Cambodia, Japan. But all the time we have shared a common dream: mainland China.

When France and Communist China renewed diplomatic relations in 1964, my boss quickly obtained a tourist visa and was off, carrying with him a list of questions I had drawn up that would help us assure the physical comfort and peace of mind of our exacting clientele. I asked about medicines, doctors, clothes, the climate in various regions, the length of time needed to travel from place to place, the availability of Catholic churches, room service in the hotels, cleanliness, hairdressers, electric voltage, arrangements for transporting large amounts of baggage, night life in the towns.

Five weeks later the boss reappeared supremely happy. He had been charmed by the little Chinese men, disappointed by the little Chinese women, and irritated by the propaganda. And, of course, he had lost my list of questions.

Before the Chinese had an embassy in Paris, I had written to their embassy in Bern, Switzerland, asking about the possibility of organizing a "cultural group tour" of China. No answer. I had then sent the same letter to the newly opened Paris embassy. At the end of three weeks I had had a brief reply asking me to write to Luxingsche, the Chinese travel bureau in Peking. I had written a third edition of my letter, in English this time. Two months later I got a reply with a superb stamp showing a rice paddy. "Agreed," it said, "but why don't you write in French?"

VI

I immediately sent off a detailed letter indicating the itinerary we hoped to follow. It was a synthesis of the trip the boss had taken, along with the results of my background reading. I insisted on visiting Loyang and Sian, two ancient cities rich in historical associations.

After the obligatory delay of about two months the reply came back with another marvelous stamp—this time showing a bridge over a mountain river, probably the Yalu. "The program is fine, except for Loyang and Sian, and the tour will start in the middle of September." I began calmly to tear my hair. I wanted Sian and Loyang. Besides, on September 15 the schools would still be on vacation and the hunting season would be imminent. We would be able to sign up only a few old people.

I wrote to Peking expressing our sincere regret: because we could not come to an understanding about the itinerary or the date, we would be obliged to give up this pilot trip, which would have cemented the indestructible Sino-French friendship.

Two weeks later Luxingsche made it known in rather wooden French that an exception would be made and that their distinguished visitors would be received at Loyang and Sian. No date was mentioned. At this point I became really nervous. We had not even begun advertising the trip.

Two and a half months later another letter came. No one was bothering about the beautiful stamps anymore. "Do not come before October 9, because October 1 is a national holiday, and Peking will be jammed during that week." It was too bad about the parade, but by this time we felt that it would be better to see Peking on the ninth than never.

We ran a splendid color advertisement in the magazine,

VII

with an evocative photograph of the Imperial City and my name in large letters, reassuring because I was a veteran of many past trips. The whole package could be had for three thousand dollars, which worked out to one hundred dollars a day. It was not to be an economy tour.

Three days later we had one hundred twenty requests for information, some accompanied by a deposit.

When some experienced travelers criticized the itinerary, I replied that I was powerless to modify it in the slightest degree. I could hardly see myself asking Luxingsche to change a single detail in the hard-won agreement.

In the end we welcomed each cancellation or hesitation. I even went so far as to urge certain of our best clients to wait until the next year, when the rough spots would have been smoothed out of the tour. We used every excuse to reduce our enthusiastic following to twenty—twenty-one at the outside. The obligatory and completely innocuous yellow fever shot discouraged eight would-be tourists. The lack of sea bathing eliminated four more. A man in the metal business and his wife dropped out when they discovered that we would not see the blast furnaces of Manchuria.

Our final list of travelers received a brochure we had written about the history of China, three little books on Chinese art, plastic baggage tags with their names printed in gold, and our blessing.

This is the story of our trip, authentic in every detail except for the names of the tourists, which have been changed. A listing of the cast of characters and of the itinerary we followed appears in the endpapers.—C. M.

VIII

1

Thirty thousand feet below our Tupolev, a few hills appeared in the distant haze, then a vast plain, and on the horizon, touched with pink by the rising sun, Peking. Two years of negotiations, one year of preparation, four days of chaotic travel, and now here was China. For a whole month I would lead the most expensive tour in the history of world travel, a tour of Communist China for millionaires. There were twenty of them who had left their hunting lodges in Sologne, their all-night revels at Régine's, their dinner parties, Rolls Royces, and fittings at Chanel's. I would lead twenty members of the European upper crust while they mixed with Mao's human ants.

I too had an old Chanel suit in my suitcase and my

car wasn't a Volkswagen. Nobody could really call me an intellectual, and my left-wing principles had been known to desert me. Nor was I a graduate of the School of Oriental Languages. The only things to draw me toward China were a fascination fed by childhood reading, a strong sense of curiosity, and an eagerness to learn all I could about that mysterious country. But oddly enough, during the next four weeks, I was to live on the frontier of two worlds, the world of my twenty snobs and the world of the Chinese people, for the latter would regard me as the "proletarian" of the group, the working girl, the industrious shepherd of an exacting capitalist flock the likes of which the Chinese had never met before.

Our Tupolev made a noisy, bumpy landing. A reception committee of Chinese buttoned up to the eyebrows in fawn or black gabardine suits was waiting impassively in the rain, clutching bunches of gladioli. A group of Yugoslavs were the first to emerge from the plane. The Chinese bowed, smiled, made speeches, listened to the replies, got rid of their gladioli, and led their visibly daunted guests away.

We got out next, before the Negro students who filled the rest of the plane. In the lounge, in front of the gigantic bust of Mao (a speaking likeness down to the wart on the chin), a smiling young man dressed in the usual high-necked gabardine uniform made a gracious speech of welcome in French. His name was Shin, and he was to be our chief interpreter throughout the tour. He was tall for a Chinese, and slim, with eyes that smiled behind his metal-rimmed glasses and long, delicate hands. Shin introduced me to Yuan, a man of about thirty who was dressed all in black. He had a long, hard face, a big nose, thick lips, and dazzling teeth bared in a perpetual smile. His little hand held mine for a long time. Then, inspecting me absently, he launched into a long mono-

2

logue, which Shin translated simultaneously into French. "The Chinese People's Republic," Yuan declared in conclusion, "is happy to welcome its French friends, and wishes them an interesting journey."

Standing in front of my flock, who had collapsed onto the arms of easy chairs or onto their hand luggage, I shifted from one foot to the other, slightly intimidated by the pompous side of this welcome. I responded by expressing our joy at finding ourselves at long last "on the soil of this great country."

To this Yuan replied, "We have the same desire you have—to make this tour a success. We want to show you everything, the things of the past as well as our modern achievements."

I seized my chance, for I had heard how hard visitors had to fight in China to see museums and pagodas instead of factories and dams. In my warmest tone I said, "Thank you, Monsieur Yuan, for greeting us with such a splendid promise, for we have come a long way to visit your country. We have an equal interest in its astonishing past, its admirable present, and its glorious future."

I hoped that this acknowledgment would end the reception ceremony and that we would at last be able to go to our hotel. I was wrong. Yuan, solidly planted on his short legs, smiled even more broadly and began again. "We have a great deal to learn from our French friends, and will regard as a mark of friendship any criticism you are good enough to make about us."

After glancing at the glum faces of my fellow travelers, I declared with verbal precautions worthy of Marco Polo that we were tired and longed for a rest.

The pretty lawn in front of the airport was covered with flowers and trees, but the weather was rainy and hot. We climbed into a very comfortable Czechoslovakian bus, which had tables provided with ashtrays and white

3

lace antimacassars on the headrests. A little Mongolian woman with irregular but attractive features, who was dressed in a pair of trousers that looked like a jacket and a jacket that looked like a pair of trousers, informed me in impeccable French that she was our second interpreter and that her name was Shu. Throughout the journey she kept her narrow eyes fixed on my face and her hands in her pockets.

The bus crossed western Peking along an avenue lined with trees planted, so Shin told me, "since the liberation." That was almost certainly true: the trees were graceful and leafy, but quite small. Huge blocks of brick and concrete buildings separated by lawns and clumps of trees stood next to older houses—little whitewashed single-storied buildings with gray tiled roofs turned up at the edges to drive away evil spirits in accordance with an ancient Chinese tradition. Shin informed me disdainfully that all these would soon be replaced by wide avenues lined with huge apartment buildings of the kind we had just seen: "Five years from now, all the old districts will have disappeared." There was not a single private car to be seen. The bus forced its way through a mass of bicycles, cycle-rickshaws, and carts drawn by a horse, a donkey, an ox, a man—or a woman. No one even glanced at our bus and its capitalist cargo.

At the sight of a cycle-rickshaw Marquis Torti, a member of the Italian contingent, yelled, "There's Communism for you! I thought it meant everyone was equal, but here you've got people getting other people to pull them."

I shivered. But Shin replied calmly that with the development of motor transport the cycle-rickshaw would gradually disappear.

The avenue was now lined with trees in blossom. A fine drizzle was falling, and the air was dappled like the light in old prints. We drove into the huge T'ien An Men

4

Square, where the gigantic processions of the First of May and the First of October take place under the benevolent patronage of Chairman Mao. The square was flanked by two enormous buildings in the Stalinist style with tall, square columns: "The People's Assembly and the Palace of the Museums," Shin announced proudly. Then we came to a district where the houses seemed to have been stuck together without any perceptible pattern. They were survivals of a past during which the reigning emperors had cared about nothing but the Imperial City, so that in the absence of an enlightened middle class capable of taking concerted action, every family had built the best house it could, resulting in anarchy.

The fatiguing journey had made us extremely sensitive to the drabness of the city and its inhabitants, who hurried impassively along the wet streets. Pedestrians of both sexes wore the same navy-blue cotton jackets and trousers; gabardine clothes were reserved for teachers, doctors, engineers, and interpreters. But both cotton and gabardine, I later discovered, were sold only in exchange for ration coupons. A worker was entitled to two cotton garments a year.

While trying to see everything, I was counting the stubs of the luggage tickets Shin had given to me at the airport. There was one suitcase unaccounted for! I had only fifty-five tickets instead of fifty-six. Again I counted the tickets I had been given in Moscow. There were fifty-six all right. Which of my pilgrims was I going to have to inform of the loss of his suitcase? In this austere country the incident was sure to assume traumatic proportions. They would hold me responsible for what had happened, and I would lose all semblance of authority. I feared the worst, for by that time I knew them fairly well. We were just beginning our fourth day together. And what days the previous three had been!

5

I had made the acquaintance of my flock at a cocktail party given by us, the tour's organizers, a few weeks before our departure. Creature comforts had been a prime topic. I had faced such questions as "What's the food like in China?" "Is it cold out there?" "Are there lots of things to buy?" A painted brunette in her sixties had even asked me whether she should take along her mink coat. Suddenly panic-stricken at the idea of trailing these ferocious socialites through the land of the dungaree, I had sought out the friendly faces: a newspaper editor's widow, the proprietor of one of the leading modern art galleries in Paris, and a mischievous-looking little man from Geneva.

At Le Bourget Airport two weeks later, I planted myself a good hour in advance at the desk of the Soviet airline Aeroflot, which was to take us as far as Moscow. The attendant adamantly refused to accept my forty pounds of excess luggage. I was taking clothes for all weathers and occasions, and I had a small library of books on Chinese art and two shoe boxes full of medicines. A uniformed, gold-braided, magnificently Slav superior ruled in my favor. After my luggage had been checked, I took up a position facing the main entrance, with a slight sinking feeling in the pit of my stomach.

The first of my pilgrims to arrive were the Chapeaus, a somewhat provincial-looking couple in their fifties. The husband, a northern industrialist with close-cropped gray hair, kindly blue eyes, and gold-rimmed glasses, was dressed in a gray checked suit with an unfashionably long jacket. His wife had short gray hair and a rather shabby camel's-hair coat. She hissed at me in a shrill, affected voice: "Good morning, mademoiselle. Are you our guide?" The "mademoiselle" cut me to the quick. I may not look my forty years, but I hate being treated as if I had been left on the shelf.

Next to arrive was Adrienne Mandois, the dark, painted shrew I had met at the cocktail party—the one who had wondered whether to take her mink coat on the trip. With her crimson ski pants and matching boots, her black wig, and her bright red lips, she still looked like a vamp of the silent screen—which is exactly what she was. She bore down upon us, simpering and smirking, trailed by two porters laboriously dragging several trolleys loaded with suitcases.

"I like to change trousers every day." She giggled.

"And boots too?" I asked amiably.

"Of course. I've got some in velvet for the evening."

"She must have varicose veins," whispered Alexandre

Dupont, the little Genevan who was to be my factotum throughout our tour.

Adrienne Mandois chattered on imperturbably. "Laure!" she exclaimed effusively, wringing the hand of the Countess de Castillat, a frail creature in her sixties who walked with a stick. Laure wore her red hair in a large chignon, and her delicately wrinkled face was lit by keen, mocking blue eyes. The Countess de Lissaye, elegant and fair-haired, dashed in, haloed with small parcels.

All of a sudden there was something like the scramble for the last train on the metro. My charges arrived all at once with a jumble of luggage. Georges Wolf, the proprietor of the modern art gallery, whose black hair was tousled like that of a wicked angel, laid five expensive suitcases at my feet in a homage I could well have done without. But the Aeroflot attendant seemed totally resigned.

Shaking hands in the midst of a pyramid of suitcases, I began to get everyone mixed up; to be rid of them I advised them to lay in a stock of whisky and cigarettes for the journey. At the last minute Aeroflot claimed that Pariet, our artistic adviser, was not booked on the flight and refused to take him on board. There were shouts and lamentations in two languages, but finally Aeroflot gave in once again.

After a terrifying, shuddering takeoff I went around fussing over each member of my flock. Marquis Torti was a lanky, charming Italian of about sixty, with a thin face furrowed by two vertical lines, a booming voice, and inexhaustible eloquence. He gazed ecstatically at his companion, the very beautiful Signora Coli, who was nearing fifty with a good figure, sculptured features, high cheekbones, and huge dark eyes. Marquis Torti had clearly appointed himself the protector of the Italian

8

minority in our group, for he was already lecturing poor Signora Leandri, a diplomat's widow, who was sipping her vodka and hiccupping happily. Within earshot of Marquis Torti was the wife of a Milanese industrialist, Signora Negri, an attractive middle-aged woman whose finely chiseled face framed in gray hair made her look like an eighteenth-century marquise. Her daughter, Isabella, in the next seat, was dreaming like a Botticelli come to life. At the front of the plane sat General de Boilèle. His pale-blue eyes, lurking behind a scrub of gray eyebrows, made him look like an old pirate. He bent his elegant height toward his friend Mme. Trollan, who in her haughty fifties was not quite the glowing beauty praised twenty years before by Parisian society. Barely acknowledging my polite greeting, she turned her magnificent head away and went on picking at her caviar.

As I continued my rounds I felt the pang inseparable from the beginning of any tour—the feeling of being alone in a lions' den.

After a brief, confused stop at Moscow we crowded into another Tupolev, this time a single-class aircraft, which was to take us to Peking. My pilgrims were scattered among students from Cuba, Ghana, and Rhodesia, who were off to study at Peking University. My neighbor, a redheaded giant who looked like an American football player, was actually a Frenchman. He never stopped laughing, lived in the United States, which he loved, and traveled every year to China, which he also loved. On the other side of the aisle, four Yugoslavs drank the last of my bottle of vodka. One of them spoke French very well and seemed most friendly; the other three lay right across him to ogle the pretty legs of Isabella Negri.

At two in the morning we touched down at Omsk, in western Siberia. A fat hostess wedged herself into the aisle and barked that the plane would not be taking off

9

again immediately. Acting on a premonition, I advised my flock to take their hand luggage with them. Some of them objected. I insisted, and they were to thank me later.

A boneshaking bus deposited us in front of a two-storied barracks. At the top of a narrow concrete staircase, we found a long corridor lined with square green cells nine feet wide, each furnished with two iron bedsteads, a washbasin, a chair, and a light bulb hanging from the ceiling. My pilgrims lost their polish; each one rushed headlong into a room. I shared with the pleasant Signora Leandri, the Italian diplomat's widow. The poor woman was tormented by the idea that she might not have time to put on her corset in the event of a sudden departure. I gave her my word of honor—shouting at the top of my voice because she was stone-deaf—that the plane wouldn't take off before she was properly corseted.

The central heating was capricious—the bedrooms were either scorching hot or icy cold—but there was a general atmosphere of gaiety. Nobody really felt like going to bed. The French ambassador in Peking, who had been on our plane, was joking with my redheaded seatmate, who had obviously taken the fancy of Adrienne Mandois. Then a tall Intourist man with crystal eyes and a tough jawline informed me in monosyllables that we would not be leaving before five the next morning because of fog over Irkutsk, our next stop. Feeling rather pessimistic, for I had rarely seen a fog lift at five in the morning, I tucked my flock in for the night. Most of the students were already asleep on camp beds in the corridors. In front of the door of my room a pretty Cuban girl was stretched out on a mattress, reading Maupassant's *Bel-Ami*. She was gay and intelligent, and after leaving her I felt a little embarrassed at the prospect of spending the night in a real bed. Before I slept, I promised my roommate that I would wake her at least half an hour before departure, to allow time for the corset.

We were awakened at eight by shouts from the Intourist representative, who pushed us, without a word of explanation, into the jolting bus of the day before. At the airport restaurant, trim waitresses in floral aprons served us a copious Siberian breakfast: borscht, brown ale, kippers, sardines with onions, chicken and mashed potatoes, and creamy yogurt. After the usual protests—"I never eat anything in the morning"—my flock proceeded to do justice to the meal. The big dining room, its tables covered with white cloths, was packed. Peasant women with flat faces, high cheekbones, and narrow slanting eyes, dressed in felt boots and several layers of full cotton skirts, held children wrapped in huge woolen shawls. The men wore shiny gray overcoats and soft caps, while the wealthier had fur hats. Most of the Russians carried huge baskets overflowing with vegetables, eggs, chickens, even live ducks. One tubby little man was carrying a squealing piglet. All these people were waiting with patient resignation for their planes. Some would fly as far as Rostov, and even Moscow, to sell the produce of their private plots of land. Here, in the vast roadless expanse of Siberia, the plane is like the bus in most other parts of the world.

Boris, the Intourist man, announced in a rumbling growl, "Fog at Irrrkutsk. Takeoff postponed," and shepherded everybody back to the barracks we had hoped we should never see again. Morale began to hover around zero. I put on a brave smile, but I too was appalled by this new delay—China had never seemed so far away. To look after these twenty de luxe and exacting tourists suddenly struck me as an impossible burden. The ambassador did his best to cheer me up: he smilingly told me that on his last trip he had been stuck at Irkutsk for four days. That finished me off.

In the golden morning air we could see the factory chimneys of Omsk smoking in the distance. When a few small planes landed at a nearby airfield, a suspicious guard appeared and brusquely ordered us to look the other way. At lunchtime we traveled out to the restaurant and back again, with Boris announcing in the same growl that he "regrrretted" that takeoff was still delayed. I began to find the joke "wearrring" thin, and my companions were getting more irritable by the hour. I begged Boris to organize a bus tour of Omsk to keep my impatient flock amused. This request brought forth an explosion of Slav fury: "Omsk is closed to forrreigners!"

Two tables of bridge solved eight of my problems for a while, but Adrienne Mandois, our vamp, kept complaining, "I'm going to have to spend the rest of my life here, that's certain. We shall never be able to get away!"

"We ought to have gone through India," moaned the Countess de Castillat. "At least the weather's fine there."

I reminded her that there had been a war between China and India not very long before and that relations between the two countries were anything but cordial.

Suddenly it occurred to me to relieve tension and drown the boredom in vodka. Boris uttered a fresh groan when I put my idea to him. Luckily, one of my charges, a French doctor's wife from Casablanca, backed me up in perfect Russian. Dear, sweet Mme. Blum! With her lovely smiling face and her long auburn hair tied in a chignon, she was the very picture of serenity. Boris surrendered to her charm and in return for forty dollars dug out four bottles of vodka. The evening promised to be more cheerful than I had expected. Signora Negri

12

promptly began to smile, and Signora Leandri was soon as red-faced as a country priest after a good meal. In the end everyone returned to his little green cell slightly tipsy and in fairly good spirits.

None of the students in the corridor had been able to wash, so I took advantage of my roommate's intoxication to let the Cuban girl use our washbasin.

At eight the next morning we were again awakened by Boris' stentorian shouting. On our return to the barracks from the familiar restaurant, a minor revolt broke out among my flock.

"We're obviously going to stay here till we rot," Countess de Lissaye insisted. "What dreadful organization!"

"Why don't we take the trans-Siberian?" asked Laure de Castillat. "You must fix that up for us."

"The trans-Siberian takes a week," I said impatiently. "You have to have reservations, and above all visas, which they can't give us here."

"We ought to go back to Moscow and wait there for the fog to clear at Irkutsk," Colette Quesnel, the newspaper editor's widow, suggested.

"We haven't got a visa for Moscow either," I snapped.

Signora Negri suddenly became a geographer. "Why don't we go through Pakistan?" she asked.

I found myself surrounded by a noisy mob as the startled French ambassador looked on. General de Boilèle beckoned me into his room. Mme. Trollan was sitting on the bed, scowling and looking beautiful. Boilèle stamped his foot and screamed, "I order you to get the group together and tell them that if we haven't left Omsk by tonight we are going back to Paris."

I suddenly lost my temper. I reminded everybody that I was the one who made the decisions here. "Now

13

that I've made that clear, if any one of you wishes to leave the group, you are welcome to do so, but you take all the consequences."

There was a profound silence. Boris summoned us to lunch. The ambassador was kind enough to take charge of Mme. Mandois, and very successfully too, to judge by her fluttering eyelashes.

A charming buxom blonde took over from Boris, who said good-by to us with a stiff bow. She completely won me over by whispering that we would be leaving after lunch. When I gave the signal for departure—at the very last moment, for fear of another disappointment—the general patted me on the back and said, "What did I tell you? I knew that everything would work out all right!"

The bus was taken by storm. Señor Neralinda, a Peruvian banker who had joined us at Moscow and who looked like a plump pullet, launched into a lively conversation with the lovely Cuban Communist, asking her countless questions about the subjects she was going to study in Peking. Adrienne Mandois was shaking her wig bewitchingly at the ambassador. The atmosphere was positively euphoric. It seemed the ideal moment to tell my flock that we would have to spend the night at Irkutsk, since the airport there was not equipped for night flights. A storm of cheers greeted this news, which only two days earlier would probably have caused an insurrection.

"It will be amusing to see Irkutsk!" they said.

I boarded the Tupolev lightheaded with relief and promptly fell asleep.

Four hours later we were slithering through the muddy snow to the dimly lighted airport at Irkutsk. Like the railway station of many a French village, this airport is situated at the end of a broad, gloomy avenue lined with trees and three-storied houses. After struggling

14

through the snow for two hundred yards, we entered the hall of the only house with lights on. A buxom lady bursting out of a black uniform with silver buttons bawled out the names of the passengers, allocating one room to every six names. How would my de luxe passengers take this, I wondered, when some of them had paid handsome sums to have a room to themselves? I exaggerated the number of my charges and obtained half a dozen extra rooms, which I shared as best I could.

I grouped the three men I privately called the Musketeers: Georges Wolf, the art gallery owner, Alexandre Dupont, the Swiss, and Georges Noiret, a little man who had once given me a bit of a headache on a tour of Egypt by trying to impress his sulky blonde companion with his dictatorial attitudes. With his pointed nose, his tiny round eyes, and his thinning hair brushed down over his forehead, Noiret reminded me of a miniature Napoleon. This time, thank heaven, he was alone, and I tried to neutralize him with a mixture of charm and haughtiness.

I chose to share a room with Mme. Adjouf, whose husband owned a great deal of land in Morocco. She had an attractive, intelligent face with squirrel eyes, walked with her toes turned out, and was forever interrupting her tubby, sweet-natured, stammering husband. I sent him off to join the Musketeers. Marquis Torti, to my relief, decided to sleep on a sofa in the huge room where the four Italian women were installed. "It's better than the Ritz here!" he said gaily.

As in Omsk, the corridors had been filled as if by magic with four lines of beds occupied by Russians. They slept almost soundlessly, the men in their singlets, the full-bodied women in their bras.

Tupolevs roared into the sky directly over our heads. I finally sank into a delightful sleep at five forty-five. At six I was awakened by shouts: it was time to get up. Bleary-eyed, I stumbled across the whole of snoring Siberia to rout my flock out of bed. A delicious breakfast expertly served at the airport restored our interest in life.

Soon after daybreak we were flying over Lake Baikal, which sparkled between chalky cliffs. The only sign of life as far as the eye could see was a camp of painted felt tents, called yurta, that belonged to Mongolian nomads. The rolling countryside was covered with sparse undergrowth powdered with snow.

I had spent a year reading about China, and now, in charge of an exacting flock, I was on the threshold of a world about which I still knew nothing. I was suddenly frightened.

For the moment the problem of China paled before the problem of the missing suitcase.

Porters were emptying mounds of luggage into the huge tiled foyer of the Tsien Men Hotel, the Hotel of Friendship, in Peking. The walls were covered with brownish velvet hangings, and scattered here and there were tables reminiscent of the twenties, each with its large thermos of hot water. To the right of the door was the reception desk, manned by a receptionist who spoke only Chinese. To the left were the post office and a bank, where the clerks also spoke only Chinese. As I gave each member of my party his room number I sent his luggage upstairs. Soon I was alone in the empty foyer. The missing suitcase was my own! Half an hour later, in a hot tub, as I gazed at the dirty, crumpled suit I had worn since leaving Paris, now my only piece of clothing, I felt two huge tears roll down my cheeks and disappear into the bath water.

My room was comfortable, even very comfortable. It had writing paper, a cake of soap, a gigantic thermos of steaming water, the little canister of green tea that we found everywhere we went, and slippers at the foot of the bed. My window looked out on a little park in which two old women were strolling. They were dressed in black tunics and trousers, their hair was done in low chignons, and their feet were bound; they were holding by the hand two tubby children in red and yellow outfits that made them look like comical peonies.

Our first Chinese lunch was pleasantly swift, which we found to be the general rule. We sat at a long table in a huge dining room and were served by girls in blue cloth trousers and white blouses; some of them had long plaits hanging down their backs, while others wore their hair short. They were completely impassive except when Pariet, our cultural guide, joked with them in Chinese. When that happened, they became individuals. One burst out laughing and became very friendly, another smiled but remained reserved, and a third pursed her lips and tried to ignore these uncivilized foreigners. The food was good and simple, a combination of European and Chinese dishes washed down with soda water and a cool, light beer. The coffee, on the other hand, was an infusion of barley or something else. Torti and the Countess de Lissaye brought out their cans of Nescafé and called for hot water with a great many extravagant gestures. Good food made us happy, true Latins that we were. From being as strange as Mars, China had suddenly become familiar and reassuring.

18

In the afternoon, on our first excursion, we stopped for a moment in T'ien An Men Square, the Place de la Concorde of Peking, which we had glimpsed that morning on our way from the airport. Nowadays in the huge, almost deserted square, there are only a few bicycles, an occasional truck, and one or two taxis, but everywhere traffic lights go on controlling a ghostly flow of bygone vehicles.

Children came trotting into the square, marshaled in groups of twenty by girls in blue. Their full, rosy cheeks and smiling faces formed a curious contrast with their absolute silence. They were dressed in blue trousers and bright-colored smocks and they formed a double chain with each child holding the smock of the child in front. Each cluster of twenty looked like a bunch of flowers on the wet pavement.

The rain stopped. We drove along broad avenues lined with single-storied houses roofed with round gray tiles. At each corner the ridge tile was turned upward. Shin informed us that this traditional style had been abandoned in the construction of modern apartment houses because of the high cost involved.

"So there aren't any demons left in the new China?" Noiret, the little Napoleon, asked maliciously.

"Oh, yes, Monsieur Noiret, there are still some demons in China, and Chairman Mao seems to have been having trouble with them lately. But I think he prefers to use more effective weapons against them than curved tiles!"

The sky was turning pink, and I asked Shin to take us to the street of the antique dealers. It was the end of the day, and crowds of people were pouring out of the offices and workshops. The women were dressed uniformly in blue cloth trousers and quilted grayish jackets; there was not the slightest coquetry in either their clothes

19

or their bearing. Their faces were expressionless, their eyes far away. But they turned around to look at us after we had gone by, and some of the younger ones burst out laughing at the sight of our shoes and stockings, so different from their black felt slippers.

The men, on the other hand, didn't hesitate to look and even to smile at us. They too were dressed in blue trousers, with matching tunics or padded jackets and identical soft caps. Like the women they wore black felt slippers, or rubber ankle boots. A typical street, we found, was spotlessly clean: there was never a single piece of paper or orange peel to be seen. The whole country seemed to have been swept clean a few minutes before we arrived.

My inquisitive flock dispersed. I went into a few little shops with wooden fronts, which were full of pretty porcelain and rather ordinary statuettes made of semi-precious stone. I was intrigued by a dealer in paint-brushes, whose shop was dimly lighted by a single light bulb hanging from the ceiling. There were brushes of all sorts—with waxed, varnished, or lacquered wooden handles, bristles that were black or white, long or short. Noticing my interest, the smiling, middle-aged owner staged an extraordinary little ballet of paintbrushes against the background of the glass showcase. I was fascinated by the Chinese characters he mimed: there was the slim, supple girl, the romantic young man, the stocky, broad-shouldered lout, the silent, white-haired old mother, and the sensible, dull-witted friend. The entire Peking Opera was suddenly and gracefully conjured up before my eyes.

The antique dealers of Peking are generally quite elderly. Most of them, Shin told us, once owned their shops. Now they are "in partnership" with the government. They are not allowed to sell anything more than

20

one hundred years old, and the prices are fixed by a government agent who puts a red seal on each article "approved as suitable for sale."

Night had fallen, and the narrow street was only dimly lighted by the time we had all returned to our bus. Everybody unwrapped and showed off his minor purchases and major discoveries. Sitting alone at the back of the bus, I felt reasonably pleased with myself, slightly bewildered, and quite uncertain about what lay before us. I suggested to Shin that on our return to the hotel we hold a conference to plan the rest of our stay in Peking in some detail.

Yuan, the gloomy, haughty-looking guide who had greeted us at the airport, led me ceremoniously into a thickly carpeted lounge on the fourth floor of the hotel. It was furnished with a settee and several deep leather armchairs arranged in a semicircle. Low tables in front of each armchair were set with tea, cigarettes, matches, and ashtrays. A bust of Chairman Mao presided. Yuan trotted out an improved version of his airport speech, expressed his admiration for my devotion to my task, and begged me to spare no criticism, for "we have a great deal to learn from our French friends." I began to suspect that this request would be one of the chief themes of our journey and that all would go well provided that I never criticized anything. Accordingly I launched into a lyrical speech about the great Chinese people, my confidence in the success of our tour, and my gratitude to his friendly team.

After Shin served tea we finally settled down to work. Yuan outlined the program for our stay in Peking day by day, with Shin translating a sentence at a time. Yuan looked at me while he spoke in Chinese and continued to look at me while I answered in French, as if we could understand each other. He had the face of a peasant,

21

of a man of action, of a fanatic who knew no doubts—in short, of the perfect Party man.

Shin's translations were conscientious and brief. I wondered whether his knowledge of French was as extensive as it appeared. I would have to make myself very clear. While he was talking I noticed his eyes, which were creased with merriment behind gold-rimmed glasses. He had a triangular, catlike face and the natural distinction of a bourgeois intellectual.

I was sitting on the settee next to Yuan, who had installed his staff on his right. Shy little Pariet sat on my left. To increase his prestige in the eyes of the Chinese and to cement our relations, I repeatedly asked his opinion.

In an excited small voice he made a number of suggestions that were anything but stupid. He was charming, even touching. In Siberia he had been a good companion and a reliable colleague. He talked enthusiastically to the Chinese; he liked them already. His liberal heart and socialist mind made this journey a real mission for him. Yuan agreed to all our suggestions almost without discussion. We shook hands warmly and said, "*Shee, shee*" ("Thank you, thank you").

Back in my room I was delighted to find some underwear sent to me by Colette Quesnel, and some clothes, unfortunately too large for me, from Mme. Blum and Mme. Adjouf. The elegant Italian women, who were just my size, hadn't contributed so much as a handkerchief. During a relaxing bath I performed what was to become the daily ritual of doing my laundry. Then I made myself a cup of Nescafé, from a can given to me by a friend who had known that I wouldn't find the Ritz in the land of Chairman Mao.

Our first dinner in Peking was at the Lacquered Duck, a restaurant on Tchien Men Wai Ta Thieh Avenue, a wide street lined with unlighted shops. Having passed through a large, bright room in which a few foreigners were dining, we settled in a private room at two round tables covered with white cloths. A well-trained headwaiter in a white jacket promptly filled our large glass with cold beer and our two small glasses with *mao-tai*—rice alcohol—and a rather sweet warm red wine.

To my horror, Yuan stood up before the meal and began to speak on his usual themes: Franco-Chinese friendship, the lessons we could teach each other, and the friendly criticisms we should make of our hosts. After this homily he toured the room with his glass of *mao-tai*, clinking glasses with each guest in turn. When he had finished he shouted, *"Kampei!"* and drained his glass at one gulp.

I stood up in my turn, and while Shin translated sentence by sentence, I embarked on a pathetic flight of oratory on the same themes and proposed to my hilarious audience a *kampei* to Sino-French friendship. Only then did the ritual of the Chinese meal begin: a dozen main dishes in rapid succession surrounded by satellite dishes, variations often hard to define but always deliciously light—sharks' fins, salads, bamboo shoots, rotten eggs, roots, leaves, stalks, chicken, and pork. Everything had been cut into small pieces and cooked only briefly.

The high point of the evening was the lacquered duck, which was displayed to the company and then taken away to be carved. It had been glazed with a paste of melted sugar, filled with water, and grilled on a wood fire, so that the outside was crisp while the inside remained deliciously tender. As an added treat we were given the duck's liver, a delicacy that would send French gourmets into ecstasies. Throughout this feast the vigilant headwaiter never let our thimble-sized glasses of *mao-tai* and red wine remain empty for more than a moment. As the guests' spirits rose, so did their voices. The Italians were particularly gay, and Torti kept fussing over the ladies on either side. Noiret, whose nose had turned red, was extremely gracious, my little Swiss seemed to be in seventh heaven, and Signora Leandri was taking on board huge shipments of *mao-tai* with evident relish. Shin was not drinking and had started giving the slightly tipsy Pariet an involved lecture on Marxism. Shu, on the other hand, was drinking hard but remained as sober and silent as ever, her eyes creased in constant vigilance. Yuan ate and drank with obvious pleasure, conscious of the rarity of the occasion and the excellence of the fare.

The conversation was a little strained. It turned chiefly on comparisons of the climates of Peking and Paris and of the rival merits of Chinese and French cooking. As soon as I asked a remotely personal question, Shin stopped translating and Yuan smiled at me uncomprehendingly. I told myself that I must be patient.

Bowls of rice were brought in, but courtesy forbade us to touch them. If we did, it would mean that the rich profusion of dishes that had been served had not been enough. I quickly passed on the warning *mezzo voce*.

Yuan brought the evening to an end by clearing his throat and spitting vigorously into his handkerchief, which he carefully put back into his pocket. My stomach turned over slightly, and I whispered to Pariet, the Sinophile, "Is that customary here?"

"Of course," he replied, with a touch of scorn for my bourgeois reaction. "In every country in the Far East people clear their throats all the time."

The meal turned out to be exceptionally cheap for our Western purses: two dollars each, or five yuans. As the average wage of a Peking worker was sixty yuans a month, it was obvious that a meal of that sort was a luxury the ordinary Chinese could seldom afford. I expressed concern to Shu about all the dishes we had barely touched, in a country where every morsel of food was carefully counted. She replied without the slightest embarrassment that as soon as we left, the staff of the restaurant would devour the leftovers like a flock of vultures.

We had all been given rooms together on the fifth floor of the hotel. A young porter handed us our keys—symbolic keys, since we always found the doors unlocked. Probably our hosts thought that keys would reassure their Western guests—and as politeness consists of assuring your guests of your good intentions, we had to have keys of some sort. "Their damned doors don't shut anyway," Adrienne Mandois commented rudely, "so what's the use of giving us keys?" But then, Mme. Mandois had little use for symbols.

Before going upstairs, each member of my group struggled with the poor hall porter trying to arrange for breakfast to be served the next morning in his or her room. But as the time and nature of the order varied from one individualist Latin to the next, I asked Pariet to intervene. He covered the porter's notebook from right to left with graceful ideograms that meant such prosaic things as "Tea at 8:00 for Room 543" or "Coffee and rolls at 7:45 for Room 521."

I opened one eye at six o'clock in the morning, cursing a concert of horns worthy of Paris in the days before driving with the horn was forbidden.

It was already light outside—a dusty golden light—and I saw that only two cars were responsible for the din. Swarms of passing cyclists rang their bells for all they were worth; a few red and blue buses drove by packed with people. In the park behind the hotel, three girls in white blouses and black trousers were forcing a young man off his bicycle and roaring with laughter.

During the morning I tried to get in touch with Charlotte Florent, a French girl who was nearing the end of her second year as a student at Peking University.

The Guimet Museum in Paris had told us that of all the French residents of Peking, she knew the most about Chinese history and culture. By letter she had agreed to act as a lecturer and guide during our stay in the capital.

At the other end of the line a metallic voice answered curtly, there was a click, and we were cut off. I tried again. Another click. Shin told me that I had to apply for permission to get in touch with a foreign student.

"Apply to whom?"

"I'll see to it myself."

"I'd like to see the official who's responsible for giving permission," I said.

"That official doesn't exist. I'll see to it myself."

I also asked him to apply to the official who didn't exist for permission to call on a Chinese doctor who had lived in England during the Second World War, when he had met one of my English friends.

Feeling skeptical about the outcome of my requests, I made successive attempts to change some money and to buy post cards and stamps. It took a very long time. The young men at the *bureau de change* were earnest, silent, and slow. The girls in pigtails who were selling post cards and stamps twittered like little birds and took out of a glass case a variety of stamps depicting Chairman Mao, flowers, landscapes, butterflies, peasants in the fields, dams under construction, factories, craftsmen at work, antiques, Chou bronzes, and T'ang vases. Philately in China is a kaleidoscopic summary of national life. The girls handed over each stamp slowly and reluctantly, as if it were a gold coin. There was no glue on the backs of the stamps nor on the flaps of the envelopes—for reasons of hygiene, according to Shin, but possibly also for reasons of economy—you dipped a little brush into a pot of liquid glue and dabbed it on. The salesgirls worked out the price of my purchases on an abacus like those we had learned to count on at school; the rapid clicking of the wooden balls delighted me. The abacus is the computer of the Far East, and ardent propagandists maintain that a skilled operator can beat a computer hands down.

My next stop was the telegraph office, where I sent off a barrage of tearful cables in an attempt to find my suitcase. Georges Wolf, the gallery owner, was there, trying to send a cable to Paris and looking positively tragic. The girl at the counter conscientiously made him spell every word of his message. I felt my toes curling with impatience. Marquis Torti loudly insisted that his cable to Milan go express, while M. Adjouf timidly tried to attract the wandering attention of one of the cable-spellers. Finally we simply left on the counter a pile of unspelled telegrams to be sent off in our absence. The poor girls, bewildered by our Latin exuberance, would have torn their hair out if such a dramatic gesture had been conceivable in China.

At five minutes to nine I started rounding up my group. Signora Leandri arrived five minutes late. Then Adrienne Mandois surfaced, wearing a golden yellow wig, blood-red ski pants, and boots to match. The whole busload was waiting for her, and I took the opportunity to tell them that from then on we would not wait for latecomers.

We drove back to the beautiful T'ien An Men Square, which we had glimpsed the day before. Now the center of the capital, it used to be only the entrance to the Imperial City. In the past, entry to the succession of courtyards, audience chambers, and palaces was forbidden on pain of death to anyone not in the emperor's suite.

The gilded pavilion from which Mao harangues the crowds on public holidays guarded the road leading to the palace. We crossed an arched and balustraded marble bridge over the canal and entered the first courtyard, which was flanked on the north by the first pavilion. The stairs and terraces of the huge courtyard were defined by carved white marble balustrades. The beautifully proportioned courtyard, which sloped gently up toward the pavilion, looked as if it were moving. On either side of the entrance to the pavilion, bronze dragons eight feet high looked down on children who were spending their day off from school sweeping the outer courtyards with long-handled triangular straw brooms. This was done to eradicate the bourgeois revisionist idea that intellectual work was superior to manual labor. For the same reasons, Shin told me, students spend their annual holidays in the fields or in a factory. Shin privately admitted that he preferred the country because of the fresh air, but he said that he thought he would probably have to go into a factory the following year. In the same way, doctors, high-ranking officers, and leading officials of the regime periodically make an effort—or are obliged to make an effort—to "regain contact with the masses" in order to avoid creating a new class-consciousness. Several years before, Chairman Mao himself had been seen throwing a few pebbles onto the site of a new dam.

To the left of the courtyard I was surprised to see a nine-foot-square plot of what looked like fresh green grass. The grass turned out to be wheat, and the patch, I learned, was the private plot of the caretaker, who was entitled to eat or sell the produce—at the official price, of course. A little farther on, other schoolchildren were pulling up grass growing between the paving stones. The pavilion, with its lofty overhanging roof covered with rounded and gilded tiles, shone in the morning sunshine. The building was supported by bare wooden columns with brick walls between them.

The pavilion was painted red. "Symbolic," sighed

Signora Leandri, her ample bosom heaving like a pair of blacksmith's bellows. The paint, of course, had nothing to do with the color of the regime: the enemies of the building were not revisionists but ants and rainstorms. In the middle of the pavilion stood a huge statue of Buddha in gilded stucco, watched over by grimacing guardians standing against the side walls under a beamed, multicolored ceiling.

A silent crowd moved past the statue: women holding children by the hand, a few soldiers wearing ugly regulation soft caps, and an ivory-faced old man with a pointed beard. All the Chinese examined us with impassive curiosity.

We had gathered around that horrible gilded Buddha while waiting for Pariet to give his little lecture. At last he came running across the courtyard, pale and breathless. For some reason he was carrying an overcoat, a camera, and a packet of film.

"Where the hell have you been? Hurry up—we've all been waiting for you," I said.

"General de Boilèle says we're going too fast for him," he panted. "He's at the main entrance and he refuses to budge until you come and fetch him yourself. He insisted on my carrying his coat. He first asked Shu to carry it but she told him that she wasn't a porter." Poor Pariet was almost in tears of exasperation.

"You aren't a porter either as far as I know. I think the best thing to do would be to dump all that stuff on this little wall in the sunshine and give us the benefit of your knowledge of the Imperial City."

For three hours we walked through almost identical courtyards and pavilions, all built along the same north-south axis so that the emperor would always be able to face south during an audience. The ridge tiles, bristling with dragons, soldiers, horsemen, and fish, stood out like

30

gold statuettes against the bright blue sky.

Pariet was a disappointment. In a monotonous staccato he trotted out an uninspiring collection of dates and unadorned facts. He was obviously afraid of annoying our Chinese guides, who were supposed to give us an explanatory lecture themselves but were clearly incapable of telling us anything except that the Imperial City had been built by the people and that it had now reverted to the people.

I tugged at Pariet's sleeve and said, "For heaven's sake give us some anecdotes, some details. Put some life into it."

Pariet's fears appeared to be completely groundless. Far from being annoyed, the Chinese eagerly noted every word he said.

All of a sudden Adrienne Mandois drew me to one side. Pursing her thick, crudely painted lips and fluttering her eyelashes as if she were the heroine in a melodrama, she informed me that she was suffering from an "intestinal disorder," that she wanted to see the embassy doctor, "not one of those Chinese quacks," and finally that it was obviously "the fault of that damned lacquered duck." I deposited her on another little wall in the sunshine.

In spite of obstacles and interruptions, we finally reached the imperial apartments, where we found some handsome pieces of lacquered furniture, some Chinese bronzes and porcelain, and a few European bronzes of no great interest. Because they had been repeatedly destroyed by fire and rebuilt, the apartments evoked none of the moving memories that haunt our European palaces. The Imperial Palace had simply been occupied by a succession of more or less ridiculous princes whose names have been lost in the cruel night of Chinese history.

Silent and somber as an imperial dragon, the general arrived at last, accompanied by the beautiful Mme. Trollan. Ignoring his rage, I shepherded my flock into the Imperial Palace Museum. A huge genealogical tree greeted us at the entrance; it began with a fish and ended with the figure of a worker wearing dungarees. The museum was crowded with portraits and statues of the emperors, including Shih Huang Ti, and of Kublai Khan and Confucius. There were Han bronzes, T'ang pottery, and wonderful Sung paintings on a gold ground, round so that they could be used for fans. Knots of schoolchildren gazed silently at the showcases. As we came out into the first courtyard of the palace, a group of men and women lined up in three files fifty yards long rocked with laughter at the sight of us. This unexpected display of hilarity amused Isabella, Dupont, and a few others, and annoyed General de Boilèle and Mme. Mandois, who asked, frowning, "What are they laughing at? They're the ones who look peculiar."

Pariet whispered unhappily in my ear, "This is impossible. I can't stand a whole month of it."

The failings of my cultural adviser prompted me to attack Shin again: I insisted that he put me in touch with the young Frenchwoman who was studying in Peking. After this preliminary and not altogether successful exploration of China's complicated history, Charlotte Florent had begun to seem a sort of life buoy. She alone could show us Peking and its treasures.

Shin finally handed me the receiver and to my relief I heard the French voice I had been expecting. She would be with us in an hour.

I had no sooner hung up than the groaning Mandois pounced again. She had spent the entire morning stuck to her little wall like a limpet to a rock. I pushed her into a taxi, which Shu sent off to the French Embassy in search of a miracle-working doctor with a cure for intestinal maladies.

With all the blandness I could muster I asked Yuan to cable Moscow about my missing suitcase, burying my request in a long, involved compliment. After having received a reply in the same style, I repeated my speech in completely different terms. All this took a good twenty minutes, but it was excellent training in mental agility and self-control.

Completely beige, from her shoes to her short hair, the messiah finally arrived—Charlotte Florent, the young Frenchwoman whose learning, I hoped, would make up for the deficiencies of my home-grown Sinologist. Off we went to the History Museum, which is in a huge white building with square columns and flat roofs in the style of the twenties—one of two monumental edifices that flank T'ien An Men Square. We began with the Stone Age and progressed through a succession of vast halls paved in marble and lined with showcases. Charlotte managed very well. Rather shy to begin with, she soon got into her stride and became precise, eloquent, and interesting. Tremendously relieved, I smiled happily at Pariet, who was hurrying toward me.

"Yuan wants to see you immediately," he said. "He's furious about Charlotte Florent's showing us the museum." My heart beat wildly as I waited. Shin looked annoyed, and Shu and Yuan looked blank.

"You were given permission to telephone Madame Florent," Yuan declared, "but not to engage her to give lectures."

"This was all arranged several months ago," I replied calmly. "Madame Florent asked for permission through the French Embassy."

"Madame Florent is a student at Peking University, and her studies leave her no time to devote to other activities."

"You must be mistaken," I answered, "seeing that she is here."

This was a blunder. Stating an obvious fact is folly in China, where obvious facts lose their factual quality, and even more their obviousness. What is more, irony is either not understood, or worse still, misunderstood.

"Madame Florent," Yuan said stubbornly, "has not been given permission either to give you lectures or to act as a guide. As a matter of courtesy you may continue the present tour, but that is all."

"Madame Florent is a friend of mine," I said. "I would like to invite her to dinner this evening."

"What you do this evening lies outside our program. So you may do what you like."

"Thank you, Monsieur Yuan," I said, "for your co-operation and understanding."

Yuan's smile, which had never changed during our argument, vanished. All the same he added, "I would like to tell you how much I appreciate your collaboration and to say once more how useful any contact with our foreign friends is for us."

Charlotte had not noticed the incident. Warming to her subject, she was speaking more loudly and her audience was enthralled. As she described the long history of the imperial dynasties, which was illustrated in the museum by a remarkable series of models, Yuan intervened. Speaking in short, naive sentences, he attacked the feudal slavery of imperial China, went on to condemn the slavery of the colonial period, and finished as usual by denouncing the after effects of these successive slaveries, which the young people of China should try to eradicate forever. Within a few seconds we had passed

34

from the mysteries of history to the certainties of the cultural revolution.

Modern Chinese history was illustrated in room after room full of photographs showing Mao and his followers during the heroic era of the Long March. Under each photograph a large inscribed panel provided an explanation in schoolroom language. Yuan prophesied that the Chinese revolution would rapidly spread to all parts of the world, notably Africa and Latin America, and declared that it was the miracle of the modern world. To my horror he then asked me to confirm his statement.

My heart sank as I saw my companions' cynical smiles. I launched into a few remarks of the most consummate jesuitry: "Yes, the revolution is a miracle, but a purely Chinese miracle, since the Chinese are one of the most courageous, hard-working, long-suffering peoples in the whole world. I doubt whether a similar miracle could take place in the steaming tropics of Africa or Latin America."

Shin translated; Yuan looked perplexed, even annoyed. He scribbled something in his little black notebook.

Yuan's cast-iron conviction that he possessed absolute truth was at once touching and irritating. In spite of the traps he kept setting for me, I took care not to contradict him in any important way.

As we walked toward the Museum of the Revolution, which houses the relics of the revolutionary struggle, I tried to evoke for my cold, even hostile westerners the heroism of the Long March and the great drama of the Chinese revolution.

I told them about the Chinese Communists in southern China, mostly peasants and all volunteers, who had begun fighting a harsh guerrilla war in 1928. Beginning in 1930, Chiang Kai-shek had launched five tough offensives against them. As a result the Red chiefs, Mao Tse-tung and Chu Teh, made a dramatic decision. They gave up their small soviet republic in the south, left a rear guard of ten thousand partisans, and on October 16, 1934, three hundred thousand strong, began one of the greatest strategic retreats in history.

The Red Army crossed southern China from east to west, turning north along the Tibetan mountains. The soldiers marched through deserts, marshes, ravines, and passes, climbed snow-topped mountains thirteen thousand feet high, camped in rain forests, and most of the time existed in appalling penury, deprived of adequate food, water, medicines, and clothes.

From then on Mao was virtually recognized as commander of the campaign. He imposed strict discipline on his troops in their relations with the local populations: no raping, no stealing, no destruction of property. He formulated eight rules, which the army sang as it marched:

1. Put the doors back in place when leaving a house (the doors, being very light, were used as bedding).
2. Roll up your mat and give it back.
3. Be polite and helpful to people.
4. Give back everything you may have borrowed.
5. Replace anything you may have damaged.
6. Be honest with the peasants.
7. Pay for everything you buy.
8. Respect rules of hygiene, and dig latrines at a decent distance from houses.

The strict rules combined with the incredible hardship led to numerous desertions. Many of the enthusiastic young men who went through the ordeal died during the constant fighting against the harrying troops of Chiang Kai-shek. At this time Mao established once and for all the tactics of guerrilla warfare:

36

1. When the enemy advances, withdraw.
2. When the enemy stops to camp, harry him.
3. When the enemy avoids fighting, attack.
4. When the enemy withdraws, pursue him.

Mao's effective political tactic was to let the good behavior of his troops convince and convert the people they met on the march. From Kiangsi province in the south to Yenan in Shensi province in the west, there was a Red zone right across China, which was to provide the Communists with a strong and faithful base on which to build the future nation.

The thirty thousand survivors of the march had had their education too. While walking nearly six thousand miles, twice the distance across America, those illiterate peasants had learned to read. Each man wore on his back a piece of cloth bearing a different Chinese character. When the man immediately behind had memorized it, the two would swap places in the line and each would have a new sign to contemplate and remember.

It took the Red Army an entire year to get to Yenan and to master the two thousand commonly used signs in the Chinese alphabet. These men were to become the base of the future Communist administration.

Mme. Chapeau, Laure de Castillat, Colette Quesnel, the Adjoufs, and the Musketeers listened with interest to the extraordinary epic. Besides, they knew at least as much about the subject as I did. But some of the others looked skeptical. After hearing of the incredible sufferings endured by the heroes of the Long March, Signora Coli pursed her perfect lips and murmured, "They didn't have to do it."

Her neighbor, Señora Neralinda, went one better by answering, "Yes, they did, the poor things. They were terrorized into doing it."

I was appalled to realize my inability to touch the

imagination of my fellow Europeans, who were just as blindly attached to their beliefs as Yuan was to his. For a moment I felt utterly discouraged—an insignificant little woman in this vast country that I found deeply moving and that I was trying to offer to these people. They had made the effort of coming here, but for the most part they were insulated from China by their Western preconceptions.

A rat-faced, pimply young man greeted us at the main door of the Museum of the Revolution. Brandishing a long pointer, he led us at a fair trot past photographs of Mao and Chu Teh at the time of the Long March and of soldiers of the famous Eighth Army, and group portraits of the first revolutionary government. Our progress was accompanied by a shrill and monotonous commentary. In the middle of the last hall a huge lighted map showed the routes taken by the various armies on the Long March, together with the dates of their engagements. Signora Negri asked how many of the men had finally reached Yenan.

"One hundred thousand," our rat-faced guide replied smartly and completely erroneously.

My heart nearly stopped altogether when the same guide admitted that he didn't know where the Long March had ended. At the risk of making our comrade guide lose face, I placed myself at the service of Chairman Mao. I was astounded that the younger generation, which was entirely a product of the present regime and had known neither the colonial occupation nor the rule of Chiang Kai-shek, did not know the history of the epic Chinese revolution.

We trailed along for another hour. I left the museum in a fury, feeling that this visit, which should have filled us all with enthusiasm whatever our personal opinions, had been just a routine lecture.

In my anger I confronted Yuan in the hotel foyer. "Are you or aren't you going to let me meet an official of Luxingsche?" I asked. (Luxingsche is the government tourist agency.)

Yuan remained silent at first, and then replied, "I don't think so, because I am the person responsible for everything that concerns your group. So it's to me that you must say anything you wish to say to Luxingsche."

I flared up. "Well, I've got lots of things to say to Luxingsche, Monsieur Yuan, and I'll tell you a few of them now."

Laure and Colette drew nearer, and the Musketeers watched open-mouthed.

"Listen, Monsieur Yuan," I said, "we have an enormous admiration for all that your country has achieved in less than twenty years. But you keep asking me for criticisms with praiseworthy persistence. Well, here's one. . . ."

Shin was quite pale. Shu had wrinkled her forehead and her nose and pursed her lips. The three Chinese encircled me; I felt as comfortable as I would have felt in the middle of a Rugby scrum.

"Will you kindly explain to me," I went on, "why you refused to allow me the help of a woman of the caliber of Charlotte Florent, who has proved her admiration for the People's Republic by devoting two years of her life to studying it, when all that you can find to give me as a guide is an almost illiterate young man, just about fit to talk to primary-school children, but certainly not to people who know the history of the Chinese revolution as well as their own."

Laure and Colette were petrified; the Musketeers, appalled. I turned on my heel and walked with dignity toward the restaurant where Shin caught up with me. "You will have your answer this afternoon," he said.

At the dinner table my troops spoke to me with a certain respect, as if the Long March had been nothing but a weekend hike compared to the battle I had just fought. Only Adrienne remained impassive, waiting until dessert to give me the latest bulletin about her intestinal disorders. She was still wearing her ski pants and red boots, but her blonde wig was beginning to look a little greasy.

CHAPTER

5

I gave Charlotte Florent an account of my tussle with Yuan.

"The fools! The cretins!" she roared. "They'll never learn! I don't give a damn—I'm staying with you!"

Impressed as I was with this vigorous reaction, I was obsessed with the idea that microphones might be hidden under the carpet or behind the bed, and I urged my compatriot to speak more cautiously.

"Dear Charlotte," I said, "two days in China have already taught me the futility of losing my temper. Naturally we would prefer to discover Peking with you who know it so well, rather than with poor little Pariet. But you know better than I do that if we insisted on having you as our guide, the Chinese would be sure to put us on the first plane back to Europe, and to expel you from the university and possibly from China. Perhaps the Chinese don't want to let us mix with foreign students so they can control the national image they try to present to tourists. Don't you think that's the reason?"

Charlotte wasn't bothering with reasons. She continued to rage at the "stupidity of the Chinese." "You might just as well try to make pigs fly," I said to myself, still wondering about hidden microphones. I finally stopped the tirade by inviting her to share our dinner. The Chinese wouldn't be present, and she could give us a lecture on the history of Peking. Coming out of my room, we bumped into two members of the hotel staff standing outside the door. It was obviously an easier method of listening to conversations than microphones.

After dinner Pariet broke down. The poor idealistic man had formed a wonderful idea of what the Chinese would be like and he was crushed to find them so inflexible. He realized too that he wasn't cut out to be a guide and that he was doing his job badly. The obtuseness and pretentiousness of my companions horrified him. He knew that he was throwing the whole burden of the journey onto my shoulders and he begged me to forgive him. I comforted him with motherly advice, words of affection, and a tranquilizer, which I passed off as a vitamin pill.

While trying to send off my umpteenth cable begging Aeroflot to find my suitcase, I ran into Alexandre Dupont, the little Swiss. He was really the funniest, most delightful companion anyone could wish. His jokes, told in a deadpan Geneva accent, always sent me into convulsions. For the moment he was doubled up with laughter himself. He had wanted to find out whether it was true, as people said, that luggage was searched in Communist countries. He had sealed his suitcase with Scotch tape before going out, and on his return the tape was gone. "That proves, doesn't it, my dear madame, that what they say is true?"

Georges Wolf approached, pointing a packet of post cards at me like a bayonet. Isabella had asked him to mail them for her. "These are dynamite!" he exclaimed. "The girl's mad!"

I read them shamelessly.

"Here," she had written, "people live in a state of terror. That is why they dare not rebel. They follow the Party line because it is impossible for them to do anything else."

All we needed was trouble with the censors. In front of my two bewildered friends I tore up the cards and put the pieces in my handbag, silently hoping that Isabella would forgive me.

6

The Temple of Heaven looked very peaceful, with its broad terraces and its dark blue tiles gleaming in the golden light of a Peking afternoon.

Yuan was smiling blandly, and the others were strolling about, laughing and talking. General de Boilèle looked optimistic, and Mme. Mandois was scratching herself. Dupont was joking with Isabella, but the way he was looking at her told me that his feelings were becoming more serious than his words. I silently hoped he would be careful. She was very nice and very beautiful, but also spoiled and coquettish. Some of our group were taking pictures; others were perched on a little wall in the sunshine. In one of the courtyards two boys

44

and two girls were skipping rope. Dupont joined in, then Isabella, the Adjoufs, and I, while the children laughed and clapped their hands. Together we organized some little games and we were joined by a few soldiers from the neighboring camp. All of a sudden, in front of the Temple of Heaven, East and West were fraternizing by playing children's games together. A few weeks later, not far from that spot, a howling mob besieged the French Embassy.

Until 1912 the emperor came once a year to the Temple of Heaven to thank the gods for the blessings of the previous year. The temple owes its name to its shape and color: it is "as round and blue as heaven." (Simone de Beauvoir once likened it to a "half-opened blue umbrella.") Struck by lightning and burned to the ground in 1889, it was rebuilt with rare timber imported from the United States, a fact that sent Adrienne Mandois into a mysterious fit of snickering. After playing for a while in the Courtyard of the Echo, we climbed the so-called Charcoal Hill, a huge mound of earth created during the excavation of the artificial lakes. From the summit we could see Peking turning pink in the setting sun. It was on this height that Li the Brave, the last of the Ming emperors, hanged himself in 1664 after a military defeat. Before he died he wrote on the lining of his garment, "A weak man of little virtue, I have offended the gods, and the rebels have captured my capital. . . . Ashamed of appearing before my ancestors, I am about to die." Emperor Li may be said to have invented autocriticism.

Descending the hillside by tree-shaded steps, I asked Shin why the People's Government continued to maintain and open to the public the monuments of the imperial and colonial eras. Was their artistic value regarded as more important than political considerations? He looked embarrassed, hesitated for a moment, and hurried off to consult Yuan. When he returned he said, "It isn't to revive a past we hate that we keep these mementos, but to show our foreign visitors and our own people things that are the work of the Chinese people and therefore their property."

I persuaded Shin to stop our bus as we passed a large pagoda I had noticed from the top of Charcoal Hill. The building had been a Buddhist shrine erected by the first Manchu emperor, and now it stood like a gigantic sugar loaf in the middle of a vast courtyard surrounded by wretched huts. Out of these huts poured a horde of women in patched clothes and rather grubby but happy and obviously healthy children. As I discovered later, in spite of great efforts education was not universal in China, and when children did not go to school their mother had to stay at home to look after them; as a result, the family had only one wage earner and sank into greater poverty. In front of each hut was a little stove that burned wood and coal and served as both cooker and radiator. The children crowded around us but Yuan refused to let us go into the courtyard and he said something that made the children move away. This was our first contact with the China of the Chinese. What we saw was poor, even very poor, but it was neither dirty nor depressing, possibly because of the gaiety of the children. This was not the poverty and sadness of India; nobody had the hollow-eyed look of undernourishment. When Signora Negri started taking pictures Yuan tried to stop her, saying that nobody had the right to film other people without their permission. But the children were so fascinated that they all began tugging at the Italian woman's coat, begging for a look through the view finder.

An exasperated Yuan hustled us back into our bus. There Shin told me, "There will be a conference on the

46

fourth floor at five-ten." The precise timing surprised me. "You're sure it's at five-ten, Shin, not five-twelve?"

He looked startled at first; then the serious, conscientious young man slowly smiled with his eyes. I could almost see this conspiratorial smile fighting through successive layers of Party loyalty, devotion to the principle of collectivity, and admiration for Chairman Mao.

At exactly ten minutes past five, smiling broadly, I entered the fourth-floor conference room followed by Pariet. The Chinese had been waiting for us for two minutes and were sitting exactly where they had sat the first day. A waiter in a white jacket served tea and then withdrew. I lit a cigarette, a Kent bought at Le Bourget, with matches from the Sheraton-Park Hotel in Washington, D. C. The funny side of the situation helped me relax a little. Yuan cleared his throat and spat ceremoniously into his handkerchief. Then he started speaking in a slow, low voice, gazing at me intently all the time and smiling his wooden smile. He went on and on and on. I puffed on my cigarette to save face. Shin was looking rather embarrassed. At last Yuan stopped. Shin stood up, pulled his chair over to my sofa, and opened fire.

"I think," he declared, "that there is a serious misunderstanding between us. Naturally everything isn't perfect in China. There are many things that remain to be done. But before the liberation we had nothing. Nonetheless we took a great deal of time and trouble preparing for the visit of our distinguished guests. We think we have received you in a friendly fashion and to the best of our ability, and we hope that you are satisfied with your accommodation. That is why it is all the more distressing for us to discover that you are angry about the incident with Madame Florent and that you consider our guides inadequate. We understand that perfectly, but as we cannot offer you any better guides, we would quite understand if you decided not to continue your journey and left China tomorrow, for example."

Shin was suffering. Yuan smiled. Shu was impassive. Pariet was choking. I lit another Kent with another Sheraton match. I offered one to Yuan, who asked if they were French. "No," I said, without further comment. I lit it for him with a Sheraton match. You could have heard a pin drop. I tried to think quickly of a suitable answer, all the while reflecting that Yuan was perfectly right. It was true that the Chinese had come a long way; what they were offering us was amazing for them and would have done credit to any fully developed nation. It was true that we were blasé, capricious visitors, ungrateful and perpetually dissatisfied. I felt considerable sympathy for this man who had gone to enormous trouble, who believed in what he was doing, and who didn't hesitate to burn his bridges when the other side asked too much. I was even strongly tempted to tell him how much I respected and admired him. But we were playing a serious game, and this wasn't the moment for extraneous, if sincere, compliments.

"Monsieur Yuan, if you haven't noticed our gratitude for your welcome and our admiration for your achievements, then a misunderstanding has certainly come between us. It is a really serious one if you haven't realized that I am far too conscious of the courtesy I owe your country and the responsibility I have assumed toward my group even to consider leaving China a day before the date set for our departure. Now please help me understand why you refuse to allow us to enjoy Madame Florent's cooperation? Has she behaved badly in any way? I beg you to be completely frank with me."

Yuan replied at length, smiling all the time and not batting an eyelid. "Your request cannot possibly be granted.

48

Madame Florent is a student at Peking University, and her curriculum doesn't allow her time to engage in other activities, even for a few days. I would like to tell you how much I admire your hard work and your sense of responsibility, and how happy we are to welcome your group. We realize that we are unworthy of receiving such distinguished visitors and that we have a great deal to learn from our French friends."

I began to squirm. "No, no," I protested.

"But we do," insisted Yuan. "What is more, we regard your criticisms as a token of friendship. We are in the process of forming strong bonds between our two countries, and it is our duty to strengthen them even further."

I thought of the remarks about China made by Adrienne Mandois and other members of my party, and this praise of our "criticisms" cut me to the quick. But I was grateful to Yuan for allowing me to save face.

"Dear Monsieur Yuan," I said, "I appreciate enormously your generous words, and in order to prove to you the strength of the bonds between us I am ready to abandon Madame Florent's cooperation. In return I presume that you will do your best to make things easy for us on our journey."

Yuan had enough tact not to look as if he regarded my renunciation as a victory for his side. He stood up abruptly, followed by Shin and Shu, and shook both my hands vigorously. "No more misunderstandings!" sighed Shin. I too stood up, shook hands all around, expressed my thanks, and walked out with all the majesty I could muster, leaving the Sheraton matches on the table.

We dined early and rapidly, thanks to the speedy and increasingly smiling service we were given at the hotel. We were going to the opera at half-past seven. The theater was packed to the doors when we arrived. The walls were bare, and the wooden seats made a tremendous clatter as we settled ourselves. When the performance began, the text was projected in Chinese script onto luminous screens flanking the stage.

The production was a very popular modern opera entitled *The Women's Squad of the Red Army*. During the rest of our stay we were to see only plays and modern operas on patriotic themes, such as the war with Japan or the struggle against Chiang Kai-shek's troops. The old operas, with their fabulous embroidered and gilded costumes, had been banned some time before. The Ministry of Culture considered that stories about emperors and concubines were not suitable subjects for a popular art form: they made no contribution to the advance of Communism and did nothing to destroy the roots of revisionism and the bourgeois spirit. The workers and above all the peasants of China, uneducated as most of them were, needed an art that was intelligible and therefore extremely simple.

The curtain rose without warning to reveal a set representing the home of a rich landowner. Powerless to help, we witnessed the agony of a pretty girl who was beaten and pricked with a hairpin by the landowner's wife. Fortunately her sufferings and ours did not last long. Rebelling against the landlord's cowardly and brutal attempts to seduce her, our heroine fled into the mountains, where she had the good luck to meet a band of guerrillas. These guerrillas turned out to be women: one of the famous women's squads of the Red Army. They welcomed the heroine, comforted her, emancipated her, trained her in guerrilla warfare, and dressed her in attractive Bermuda shorts and a pretty cap. The audience wriggled happily in their seats, laughing and giggling. But nobody clapped.

After an intermission, during which we were segregated from the rest of the audience, the curtain rose on tropical rivers and palm trees. Partisans were learning to shoot by firing at a wooden effigy of Chiang Kai-shek. Inspired by revolutionary zeal, our heroine made a monumental blunder: she started a fight that turned out badly for the guerrillas. But she did her autocriticism and was given another chance. After some re-education she returned to the fold. So much for individualism, even when it was well meant.

During the second-act finale, a choir of women dressed in khaki sang underneath a fluttering red flag. The choreography of the dances was Western in style and rather sweet and simple, with an obvious Soviet influence in a dance of partisans. Something of the old Chinese tradition was still evident in the feline grace of the dancers' movements.

The contrast between the women on stage and those in the audience was striking. The latter wore clothing rather than clothes, no make-up, and a uniform barber's bowl hair style. The girls on stage, on the other hand, wore face powder, rouge, and lipstick. Their bodies were delicate, their gestures lively and graceful, their costumes rich and silky. Actors, acrobats, and dancers are selected at primary school; they receive special training, and form a privileged class that enjoys a far higher standard of living than the rest of the population. They alone are allowed to have high-quality clothes and cosmetics, which are luxuries in China. It was obvious that the majority of poor, working-class women in the audience had neither the time nor the money to think of themselves as women. Moreover, the Spartan virtues preached by the new regime clearly discouraged flirtation, a fact that seemed to distress some of my companions. At the sight of the dancers, Noiret uttered a series of frustrated clucking noises and nudged a hilarious Dupont in the ribs. Marquis Torti declared that he found these "little

51

Chinese girls absolutely charming," and M. Blum radi-
ated joy, while Georges Wolf looked gloomy and criticized the choreography. Adrienne Mandois scornfully
shrugged her shoulders and kept repeating, "In Paris
they would be hissed off the stage."

Unable to stand these muttered criticisms any longer,
Noiret and I went to sit next to Shin during the third act,
so that we could listen to the literal translation of the
libretto, which he supplied in a stentorian bellow. Nobody
around us raised the slightest objection. Feeling slightly
embarrassed, I thought how exasperated I was by the
mere rustling of a candy wrapper in a Paris movie theater. I whispered a slangy version of Shin's translation to
Noiret, who could barely sit still for amusement.

After loudly applauding the victory of the revolutionary troops, we left the theater with the silent blue-
clad audience. I myself felt sadly proletarian as I walked
home in the rain dressed in my solitary suit, which was
beginning to smell like a wet dog.

It was a bright, sparkling, sunny day, with a cool breeze—normal weather, I was told, for October in Peking. Our bus left the capital through the old Tatar quarter in the northwest on an excursion to one of the world's most remarkable monuments, the Great Wall of China. The clean, narrow streets were lined with old gray single-storied houses with roofs of round gray tiles turned up at the edges. Outside the narrow wooden shop fronts were displays of baskets, apples, persimmons, nuts, vegetables, loaves of bread of various shapes, enamelware, and simple, attractive pots painted with flowers. Women passed with bulging shopping bags, and cyclists sped by, ringing their bells. Men and women

53

were pulling wooden handcarts, carrying heavy baskets at the ends of long bamboo poles balanced across their shoulders, or pushing their children along in little bamboo carts. Soon there were fewer houses, and before long the bus was climbing hills turned to gold by autumn foliage.

After an hour's drive we descended to the north-western plain, where there were scattered cornfields and groves of apple and persimmon trees. Then another winding climb, and at last we reached the Great Wall. Hemmed in by round, rocky, wooded mountains, it looked like a fabulous serpent coiling across valleys, hills, and mountains, occasionally throwing up a square tower toward the sky before plunging into a sheer mountain pass. I was struck dumb by the grandiose beauty of the scene and was appalled to think of the three hundred thousand prisoners of Emperor Shih Huang Ti who had built the Wall. In the third century, thanks to this two-thousand-mile barrier, Shih Huang Ti had been able to repel the invading Huns, who fell back to hurl themselves on Europe instead.

I started to climb a tiny part of the Great Wall, while my companions scattered in different directions according to their inclinations and their mountaineering abilities.

The Chapeaus held hands, gazing across the landscape to the first of the Manchu hills, which were powdery blue in the distance. Countess de Lissaye went to have a beer at the Great Wall Refreshment Room. Dupont made up a climbing party with Isabella and her mother. The Blums got other members of the party to take photographs of them with their own camera. Noiret kept shooting me with his Leica., "to have something in the foreground," and the Adjoufs just smiled admiringly.

While walking slowly back to the village, overwhelmed by the beauty of the scenery and the limpid air, I stopped in front of an old woman and a young man, probably her son, who were eating little loaves of sesame on the stone steps of the Wall. They both smiled and the young man said something in Chinese. A vague intuition led me to reply, "*Faguo*"—("France"). I saw from his blank look that the word meant nothing to him. He went on speaking to me quietly. Then my intuition deserted me, and I could only smile back at him.

The old woman's feet had been bound in childhood: they were encased in tiny white cotton socks and doll-sized black felt slippers. After all Chinese women of her age have died, there will be no little feet left in China, for the appalling custom of binding girls' feet has been forbidden since the revolution. She roared with laughter at the sight of my nylon stockings and casual shoes.

We lunched very well in a bare restaurant at the foot of the Wall. It was extremely cold and we all had on several layers of sweaters. For once Pariet treated us to an excellent lecture on the geography of China, drawing a superb map from memory. Shin took notes and translated the lecture in an undertone for Yuan, who looked most admiring. When Pariet had finished, the Chinese shook him warmly by the hand. Our interpreters seemed really happy when the opportunity to learn was offered them—provided, of course, that the explanations agreed with the Party line. Much to my surprise, my flock had listened most attentively to Pariet's talk. Only the countess had nodded a little—probably the beer.

An hour's drive brought us to the tombs of the Mings. The plain, barred on the horizon by the gray and purple mountains we had just left, was crossed by a dead straight road lined on either side by a row of gigantic statues: dragons, elephants, tigers, hippopotamuses, horses, and guards in breastplates stood ten yards apart along the ceremonial way leading to the great hillside tomb of the emperor. At the entrance was a temple intended for anniversary ceremonies, and two kiosks built for the dignitaries who sealed the tomb and who were then executed to prevent them from divulging the exact site of the body.

The great vault was a huge room of splendid proportions that has been considerably restored. Inside were some enormous white porcelain vases, beautifully decorated with flowers, in which oil for the lamps used to be kept. The sight of these vases suddenly brought back the memory of a similar though less beautiful vase in my parents' house. At every childhood birthday party I had, one of my friends could not resist hiding in it, and the vase was invariably shattered. After the party I was given a spanking, and the vase was glued together again until the following year.

In a small rectangular pavilion nearby, the objects found in the tomb were displayed to the public: gold ingots, lumps of jade, bronze vases, and jewels belonging to the empress and the concubine. I was particularly struck by two vases of a special yellow hue—the funerary color of the emperors—and also by a perfect jade goblet. Marquis Torti seemed to share my admiration and told me that he had a large collection of Chinese *objets d'art* at Turin. Outside, the mountains were turning fawn, the sky pink, and the leaves red. Two girls in white bonnets were weighing wooden buckets full of large orange persimmons.

Back at the hotel Shin joyfully announced that I had obtained an appointment with the Chinese doctor whom an English friend had suggested I visit. Shin added, with a shade of respect in his voice, "Dr. Wong is a very important man. He's a member of the Consultative Assembly."

I made a strange discovery when I returned to my room. The bottle of perfume I had left on my bedside table had disappeared. A moment later I found it carefully tucked away in my handbag. The hotel staff certainly took an interest in their guests.

We had drinks and dinner with the Fayets. He was first secretary at the French Embassy, a tall, good-looking man with flashing eyes. He had spent his childhood in China and spoke Chinese fluently. He adored this people among whom he had countless friends he could no longer see for fear of compromising them with the regime. They would have to ask permission before seeing him and would subsequently have to make a detailed report of everything said and done during their visit. In addition to the considerable inconvenience, they might also find themselves on a list of suspected persons. It was not a prospect likely to appeal to anybody, however warm their feelings of friendship. M. Fayet's fourteen-year-old son went to a Chinese school and spoke the language as fluently as his father. He loved his school and had told his parents that he would not leave it, even if his father were posted to another embassy. He had made some very good friends, but outside school he was allowed to meet them only in the street.

We began discussing the Chinese passion for drawing up reports and putting everything into writing—a passion that originated in the Confucian cult of ancestors, in which the biography of great uncle No. 3 or of a fourth cousin twice removed was inscribed in detail on tablets and then placed in the hall of ancestors for posterity. On this subject our host told us a story.

Two years before, the French cultural attaché had returned to France on leave. He had a German shepherd he was very fond of, and as he could not take the dog with him he left it with the Fayets. One day M. Fayet was summoned to the Foreign Ministry, where an official gave him an extremely unpleasant reception and told him that he would have to get rid of the animal immediately. Surprised at being called to the ministry for such a trivial reason, the diplomat replied that he could not comply since the dog did not belong to him. He was curious, however, to learn the reasons behind the demand. The official then read him a four-page report establishing that the animal had knocked over a child two weeks earlier; that three years before, not far from the Old Wall, the dog had pursued a soldier of the People's Army, forcing the man to hide; that on the third of September the following year, in the village of Tien-Chi, the dog had chased the hens of an agricultural commune; and that a few months later, the brute had attacked an entire Chinese family. The representative of the French government could not fail to understand how harmful such incidents were bound to be to Franco-Chinese relations. . . .

I was excited at the prospect of meeting Dr. Wong. Shu had ordered a taxi for me, or rather for both of us. A new Shu got into the car with me—a smiling, friendly girl. She had taken her hands out of her pockets and she talked in a completely relaxed way. She told me that she was twenty-four and that she was engaged to be married in a few months. She said that in order to limit the population explosion, apart from artificial methods of birth-control, Chairman Mao advised women not to marry until they were twenty-five and men to wait until they were thirty. Sexual relations outside marriage were absolutely forbidden. Public displays of affection outside marriage were likewise prohibited and were considered

unseemly even between married couples—a case of traditional Chinese modesty reinforced by the austerity of the
new regime.

Shu and her fiancé met every evening at their local
club, where they watched films or took part in political
education meetings. There were dances too at the club,
but Shu confided that she didn't like dancing. When I
asked her whether it was her fiancé's good looks that had
drawn her to him, she replied like a child reciting a familiar lesson: "Good looks are unimportant. I noticed my
future husband because he obeys the rules laid down by
Chairman Mao, because he knows Chairman Mao's writings by heart, and because he is a good citizen."

Listening to Shu, I thought of my own daughter, who
was not quite fourteen and was mad about pop music
and long-haired boys. Shu's mother obviously didn't have
my problems.

I decided to press her harder. "I can understand that,
Shu, but isn't there something else?"

She said nothing, but a mysterious smile softened
the lines of her impassive little face. I asked no more
questions.

The taxi drew up in the courtyard of a modern three-
storied building that stood in the middle of a vast park:
the Cancer Hospital, built in 1958. I waited for a few
minutes in an immaculate yellow hall with a linoleum
floor while dozens of patients went by on their way to see
a doctor. Naturally they did not look well, but they were
all clean and neatly dressed in the regulation navy-blue
cotton. A tall, bespectacled young man dressed in gray
trousers and a beige sweater over an open-necked white
shirt came to collect me. He looked like an American
university student. He courteously led me along fawn-
colored corridors to a small drawing room furnished with
a sofa, some deep leather armchairs, and a low table laid

60

with tea bowls. From the wall a benign Chairman Mao smiled down at us. An orderly in a white smock served the usual pale tea with some slightly nauseating green vegetation floating in it.

Dr. Wong appeared in a surgeon's smock and skull-cap, his cotton mask hanging under his chin. He was a rather portly man with a florid complexion, a broad smile, and an air of energy and gaiety. He shook hands warmly, apologized for having kept me waiting, explained that he had a great deal of work, and sat down beside me on the sofa. Speaking in French, he asked about Penelope, our English friend, and her five children. I replied in English, knowing that Shu would not understand. He then talked to me in English about his three children. When he got to the second, Shu muttered a few words in Chinese. He listened to her politely, and still speaking English, said to me, "I'm afraid that your interpreter doesn't understand English."

I asked whether that meant that we had to speak French. Ignoring my question, Dr. Wong smilingly continued—in French. The gaiety of his attitude contrasted sharply with the seriousness of his eyes. I found him intense, radiant, and extremely likable. To my surprise, he invited me to dinner at his house that very evening. I replied that I was delighted by his invitation and asked whether I shouldn't get permission before accepting it. With a slight note of irritation he exclaimed, "Good heavens, no! Can you come about seven, because we go to bed early."

I was overjoyed at the prospect. To dine with a Chinese family would be a unique experience, and I knew I could talk frankly to Dr. Wong. Perhaps the doctor, accustomed to meeting European specialists on account of his Western background and medical career, was not subjected to the same surveillance as his fellow

61

countrymen. I had reached this point in my deductions when Shu got up and quietly left the room.

The conversation began to drag; I sensed that the doctor had grown a little tense. I bravely went on talking at random, hoping that our meeting would not have to come to an abrupt end.

Shu returned after a few minutes and spoke to the doctor in Chinese. He gave a curt little nod and frowned.

"I'm terribly sorry about this evening," he said. "Your interpreter tells me that you have to go to the opera. It seems that it's going to be very interesting."

There was a silence. I felt suddenly upset that this learned man, with his open-minded outlook and rich sense of humor, had to put up with such infuriating restrictions. No doubt his bourgeois origins would forever make him a doubtful quantity in the eyes of the regime. However great his skill and devotion, the Communists would always suspect him of deviationism and bourgeois revisionism. A sort of mental claustrophobia overwhelmed me as I realized that they were right. A foreign education and a cosmopolitan upbringing do not predispose a man to unconditional intellectual submission, even if that man has freely offered everything to the cause of the revolution.

Dr. Wong must have guessed what I was thinking. He continued in a gentle voice, "Don't upset yourself on my account. My life here is naturally very different from what it was in England, where I lived like an English gentleman. I ran a clinic, had my tea at four o'clock, and finished work at five. But at the end of the war against Japan the public health situation here was so disastrous and the shortage of doctors so acute that I came back to place my skill at my country's service. Under the Chiang Kai-shek regime there was such corruption and waste that any individual effort was lost like a drop of water in the sea of misery that covered China. As you are probably beginning to see, an immense amount has been achieved since the liberation. Obviously a great deal remains to be done. So you see, it is a great source of satisfaction, perhaps the greatest of all, to feel that one is being useful to one's people."

In the light of this ardent faith, the surveillance of an interpreter and the other restrictions could only seem unimportant to a man who had deliberately given up a pleasant, easy life in the West.

The doctor asked the man who was serving tea to bring the duty photographer to immortalize our meeting. Then he stood up abruptly and offered to show me his office. I guessed that this was an attempt to shake off Shu. But she trotted behind us like a faithful dog and stationed herself in the doorway of a small room where the doctor sat down at a desk littered with files and papers. I sat in the only armchair. Dr. Wong took two small rolls of paper out of a drawer. They were pictures by a modern artist, and he asked me to give one of them to the English friend who had suggested I call on him. Then, tipping back in his chair, he resumed the conversation in French. He asked me whether we might have any mutual medical acquaintances. I thought immediately of a delightful man—a Communist—whom I sometimes see at Saint-Tropez, where he owns a house. I mentioned his name on the off chance that it might mean something to Dr. Wong.

"What!" he exclaimed. "You know X!" And turning to Shu, he added, "He is a very great French specialist!"

Shu looked at me respectfully. A little embarrassed, I explained that I had met the man in question on a friend's yacht and I mentioned the name of a man famous in the Communist world.

Wong listened to me with a mischievous smile and repeated, "On Y's yacht?"

Then I asked, "Do you ever take a holiday?"

"No, never," he replied, serious again. "There's too much work to be done and there aren't yet enough doctors in China. We can't desert our patients."

We went on talking like a couple of friends. I told him that my stay in China would change my reaction to international events. He then admitted how disturbed he was by the intense reactionary propaganda in Europe that depicted China as an aggressive, warlike country.

"In fact," he said, "the only problem that preoccupies us today is the task of feeding, housing, clothing, caring for, and educating seven hundred million people. A war would wipe out the gigantic efforts we are making. It would be an absolute disaster."

He repeated the word "disaster" several times. I tried to reassure him. "Europe isn't afraid of China. On the contrary, your country arouses immense interest in Europe, and countless books, articles, and lectures are devoted to it. Only our extreme right-wing die-hards believe that China would want to start a third world war. Of course in the United States the situation is rather different."

Dr. Wong stiffened. It was obviously a delicate topic, at least in the presence of a third party. Shu's presence made it impossible to continue our conversation, so I decided it was time to go. Dr. Wong told me how much he had enjoyed our meeting and the "breeze from the outside world" that our conversation had brought him. We shook hands warmly before I got into the taxi; he expressed his regret at being unable to entertain me at dinner, begged me to call on him again if I returned to China, and waved until the taxi had driven out of the gate.

64

I was quite shaken by this incursion into an existence that was so close to mine and yet so unfamiliar.

"What an interesting man!" I said to Shu.

"Yes," was her only reply.

Did she have no opinion of her own? Or was Wong regarded as indispensable but untrustworthy? It was impossible to tell.

On the way back to the hotel I dropped in on Mme. Fayet, who had kindly offered to lend me some light clothes for the next stage of our journey in the south.

A group of delightful Chinese children dressed in peony-colored clothes followed me, laughing, waving, and shouting, "*Nikao!*" ("Hello!"). Shu spoke to them, then explained to me that they were happy because they were greeting a "foreign friend of the Chinese people." I swore under my breath. Did everything have to be explained, from the heat of the sun to the gaiety and friendliness of children? But despite it all, I was becoming quite fond of Shu. All of a sudden she asked me what I thought of the Chinese and listened attentively when I said that I liked them very much and found them intelligent, subtle, lively, and courageous. I then asked her whether as an interpreter she had noticed any differences between Western tourists according to nationality. She smiled.

"Oh, yes," she said. "The Italians are the most difficult of all. They grumble all the time and are hardly ever satisfied. The Germans are serious and very conscientious. The French are polite and very amusing."

I rejoined my flock at the Summer Palace. They had visited a series of delightful monuments with ethereal names—the Temple of the Recumbent Buddha, the Temple of the Blue Cloud—which seemed to have left them with an impression compounded of sunshine, pink walls, blue tiles, airy prospects, and exhilarating walks among mementos of the formidable Empress Tzu Hsi. For at the Summer Palace, in that maze of countless gloomy, low-ceilinged little rooms full of furniture, silks, and *objets d'art*, there roams the ghost of that one-time courtesan who, among other charming habits, used to strangle her lovers once they had served their purpose.

A pretty walk along the shores of the silvery lake, past the boat she had built of marble—with funds intended for the Chinese Navy—brought us to a pavilion where we had a pleasant lunch washed down with cold beer. Odile Audiffret, the wife of one of the attachés at the embassy, was with us. She knew the history of Peking in detail and recounted it with irresistible charm. Marquis Torti and the Musketeers were lost in admiration, and even the women thought her a "sweet little thing."

We crossed the gray, silky lake in the golden afternoon light on board long wooden boats with red latticework stanchions. Each boat was rowed by a single silent man. The hills all around seemed to melt into a mysterious mist, and the only sound was the dipping of oars into the water. This magical moment of peace was suddenly shattered by Adrienne Mandois yelling, "This outing is a dreadful bore! Let's go and do the antique shops!"

Immediately complaints erupted from all the other boats.

"I want to buy some *mao-tai*," Signora Leandri announced in her Germanic accent.

"I'm cold," howled the general.

I shut my eyes in exasperation, but the hills echoed their litany: "Antique shops . . . antique . . . antique . . . an . . . tique."

When I had recovered some of my composure, Odile asked in a whisper, "Are they always like this?"

"Usually worse," I replied.

Astonished by their visitors' capricious behavior, the

66

Chinese rowed for shore. The disembarkation was a perfect example of the Latin temperament at its most unruly—the shouts, screams, shoves, tumbles, and exclamations bore the personal stamp of the tourist trying to be first on land. The Chinese rolled their eyes at this splendid demonstration of individualism, and Odile turned to me to say, "I'm staying with you. I haven't seen anything like this for two years. Can I do anything to help?"

No, I told her; all I could do was wait for it to blow over. After they had come ashore—without giving me the pleasure of seeing one of them fall in—they refused to get into the bus. Laure and Colette asked for a taxi to go to the Friendship Shop—the big local department store. The Musketeers said they would like to "do the antique dealers," also by taxi. Signora Coli had an appointment with a friend at the Swedish Embassy. Adrienne Mandois's intestines had broken down again. Mme. Blum insisted on returning to the Imperial City—by taxi. They were shouting, gossiping, changing their minds. Finding half a dozen taxis at a moment's notice outside the Summer Palace was, I discovered, almost as difficult as arranging for a helicopter to land in the middle of the Place de la Concorde.

Between two howls from General de Boilèle I managed to get them all into the bus by promising to drop each of them off on the way. I got in last, lit a cigarette, and stolidly refused to answer the subsequent bombardment of whens, hows, and whys.

Our first stop was an antique shop. Boilèle and Georges Wolf raced each other for the best bargains. By the time I entered, the three small rooms of the shop looked like a fire sale. The showcases in the first room housed a dusty collection of bull's-blood vases, willow-green bowls, and white porcelain decorated with flowers.

In the next room Colette and Laure were picking out the best of hundreds of snuffboxes in every color of the rainbow. Hands eagerly grabbed up ivory sampans and pagodas, and statuettes in jade, carnelian, quartz, and crystal. A fever of buying seemed to have taken hold of my tourists.

Mme. Blum, whose son was an expert on Chinese antiques, was arguing with Noiret about the value of the carnelian statuettes. Mme. Chapeau was clutching an ivory figure of a fisherman. In the heat of battle each person was clinging to his finds, terrified that his neighbor might try to appropriate them. Torti flew into a temper because Blum had bought a beautiful jade plaque that Torti had chosen for himself. In one corner of the shop the Musketeers were buying dozens of knickknacks to give as Christmas presents. Señora Neralinda, the plump little Peruvian banker's wife, whose purchasing mania had never struck me before, was indiscriminately amassing piles of odds and ends. The clerks looked haggard as they beat a feverish tattoo on their abacuses. Five-yuan (two-dollar) notes, the largest denomination in circulation, were brought out in handfuls. The small, round, paper-wrapped packages looked like so many water lilies. I had to rescue my pilgrims from their frenzy literally by force. It was an operation that took some time. I thought we were all back in the bus when little Neralinda came running along, almost hidden under dozens of parcels; his wife's green eyes lighted up with excitement. They all expressed astonishment at the low prices they had paid, and at last, as we drove on, allowed themselves the luxury of admiring what their neighbors had bought.

Our next stop was the People's Market, to the northwest of T'ien An Men Square. It was a huge covered network of alleys lined with little shops displaying quilted jackets and secondhand trousers, singlets (the only undergarment that exists in China), black felt slippers, rubber boots, glazed pottery and delightful floral porcelain, fur hats, and coats of rabbit, fox, sheep, and mink (of a peculiar yellow). I tried on a mink coat and found myself looking at the reflection of Gloria Swanson in the dealer's mirror.

My little band scattered in all directions. Some disappeared into another antique shop. The Italian women invaded a wig dealer's stall, where for a few yuans the brown-haired Señora Neralinda became the owner of a superb ebony wig. "I'm going to have it dyed in Paris," she said delightedly. I must admit that the heap of spotlessly clean scalps made me feel slightly sick.

We roamed happily all over this flealess flea market. Bicycles cost one hundred twenty yuans (about fifty dollars). Piles of old tires were being cut into sandals by silent craftsmen. The stallkeepers were all smiling, helpful, and discreet and came up to us only if we stopped. The alleyways were quite crowded: the men were looking, and the women were buying with coupons and stuffing their purchases into white string bags. There were stalls displaying apples, persimmons, vegetables, little pies, and all kinds of bread; there were also kitchens where you could buy soup in little porcelain bowls with matching porcelain spoons. Then the sun turned red, the shadows purple, and darkness spread gradually over the People's Market.

CHAPTER

9

The next morning we were to travel by train to Loyang. At half past five I went along the corridor knocking on each door, and the responses were most revealing. At dawn self-control and the veneer of breeding are in abeyance, and there is nothing to mask grumpy, peevish, or downright shrewish characters. The good-natured, on the other hand, are as good-natured as ever, and friends seem friendlier. Dupont actually joked with me, and Claire Adjouf greeted me as if she had been waiting for me to make her day.

We left the hotel at half past six. The citizens of Peking were doing calisthenics as they walked to their shops and offices. Cyclists in compact groups pedaled

70

along silently while loud-speakers played snatches of Western military marches and propaganda speeches on every possible variation of the theme "Chairman Mao is our guide and savior."

The station, erected in 1950, had marble floors and pillars and even a red carpet leading to the platform between two rows of flowering shrubs. We were firmly guided toward our private car, which two men were washing and sweeping. Nobody would be allowed to pass through the car except the conductor, and the same procedure, with few exceptions, was followed throughout our stay in China. Each compartment contained four bunks already made up with delightful flowered satin eiderdowns and white sheets buttoned down on the underside. On a table between the two lower bunks were an ashtray and four white porcelain teapots decorated with blue flowers.

Boilèle started shouting that we should make sure our luggage was on the train. Everybody picked up the scent and began running up and down the corridor baying in alarm. The luggage was of course where it belonged, at the end of the car. The Chinese are so honest that they will run after you with the torn stocking you have thrown away, the empty pillbox abandoned on the dining room table, even the Sheraton Hotel matches I left behind after the famous conference with Yuan.

Before long a toothless attendant dressed in blue put a spoonful of green tea in each teapot, and another attendant, who had a great many teeth, filled the teapots with hot water from a copper watering can with a long spout. Then a woman in blue with her hair done up in a white scarf started frantically sweeping the floor, stirring up clouds of coal dust (all Chinese trains run on coal). Attendants continued to materialize at the same rate all day long. At seven in the morning loud-speakers

71

in every compartment began to expound the thoughts of Chairman Mao. As we were unable to benefit greatly from this broadcast, and as we were the only people in the car, Shin agreed to switch off the sound. The day passed in a gentle routine of social calls, conversations, reading, and dozing. The scenery was very strange: high hills of sepia-colored loess, the fruitful alluvial soil of China, cut into squares and separated by straight corridors—not a single tree, not a single road, and hardly any houses. Here and there were villages of dried-mud huts with thatched roofs. The larger houses had roofs of round tiles, but there were no turned-up ridge tiles: the region was too poor. Cultivated fields on the hillsides were few and far between. On the paths an occasional cart could be seen, pulled by a donkey, a man, or a woman. There were a few pigs and hens routing about or pecking at the ground, but no sheep or cattle, for pasture land is a luxury the Chinese cannot afford. Nor did I see any dogs—but dogs are a delicate subject in China because Westerners maintain that they were all eaten during the great famines of 1946, when millions of people starved to death. If you speak of the disappearance of the dogs, the Chinese become indignant or change the subject.

When the temperature started rising I switched on the ventilator in my compartment. I soon discovered that it worked only ten minutes an hour, like the little bedside lamp.

About eleven o'clock the train stopped at Anyang, a little Bronze Age town that has recently become a thriving industrial center. We all got out and entered a red station decorated with colored murals and crowded with market stalls selling cakes, loaves of bread, superb apples and other fruit, and paper flowers. Each stall was surrounded by swarms of Chinese travelers, who stared at us inquisitively. There were many young men in dungarees and soft caps; a few families, the youngest children firmly strapped to the backs of their mothers or elder sisters; and soldiers in indistinguishable uniforms, all external signs of rank having been abolished in 1965. The soldiers we met everywhere in China behaved with the same calm courtesy as the civilians. The luggage of the other travelers consisted chiefly of pretty, fragile wicker suitcases, or bundles hanging from the end of a pole carried over the shoulder. The gabardine-clad Party officials, whom we saw occasionally, carried plastic suitcases. During our stop at Anyang, railway workers gave our train an energetic wash.

Isabella was busy trying out her charms on Shin. The Mandois's wig was sparkling in the sunshine. The Musketeers filled my arms with apples, paper flowers, and little cakes and ogled the Chinese girls, shouting, "Look at that one! What a knockout!" You had to have a sharp eye or be sex-starved to find any beauty in these short, stocky women with their badly cut hair, shapeless trousers, and neglected complexions. Heavy work has turned the dainty little Chinese girls of the Western imagination into sexless creatures who stride along like Grenadier Guards, with their hands in their pockets. None of them returned the Musketeers' lewd glances.

For the first time, on that station platform, we had the impression of being at the very heart of China. About one o'clock in the afternoon we stopped again. Shin made us get out and led us to the restaurant car, where with many apologies for the inadequacy of the dishes, we were served a good Chinese lunch on flower-decked tables. It was very hot and the windows wouldn't open, so we lunched quickly. I asked permission to walk back through the train to our car, only to be told that we would have to wait until the next stop, at half past three. I tackled Yuan with a long homily in the Chinese manner, full of

73

compliments and apologies, explaining that we were un-accustomed to the climate, that we were suffering from the heat, and that if need be I was quite capable of pulling the alarm signal to stop the train. For the first time I had the feeling that Yuan's smile was genuine. He launched into a flood of apologies about the climate, our sufferings, the unworthiness of the meal, and the discomfort of the car. He concluded by saying that much remained to be done, that he would do his best to meet all our criticisms, and that of course he gave us permission to walk back to our compartments.

Chinese railways appear to have two classes. In the first-class carriages each compartment is separated from the corridor by a curtain and has four bunks without mattresses or eiderdowns. Whole families were crowded together in these compartments, the men in singlets, the women nursing their babies. The passengers' washcloths hung in the corridor above a narrow shelf that held enamel tea bowls.

The second-class passengers sit in pairs, face to face, on wooden benches separated by tables on which rest tea bowls. The general impression was one of over-crowding and poverty, but everything was clean and there were no smells. Pariet told us that the absence of any physical odor among the Chinese was due to the shortage of fish and meat in their diet. But it is also worth noting that cleanliness is one of Mao's commandments and is regarded as a national duty.

We were crossing the fertile Hopeh plain, which was covered with cornfields and nurseries protected from the wind by semicircular stone walls. The fields bristled with memorial stones—vestiges of the past that the government had tried to remove in order to increase the arable area. But there had been such opposition that it had been forced to abandon the attempt. I caught sight of a group

74

of six peasants pulling a wooden plow while a seventh man kept the plowshare moving in a straight line.

The afternoon dragged on, hot and sticky. To relieve our boredom Pariet gathered us together in three compartments and gave us a little lecture on northwestern China—the Shansi and Shensi provinces toward which we were traveling. He said that Shensi, the destination of the Long March, had always been the great bastion of Chinese Communism. In the first months of its existence the People's Government had accordingly set out to irrigate, equip, and industrialize that undercultivated and underpopulated region. First it had extended the railway from Peking to the province of Sinkiang, which was rich in minerals, and transferred to that province thousands of people who were starving in the overpopulated rice fields of the southeastern coastal areas or in the slums of Shanghai and Canton. This draconian policy had been aimed at establishing a better distribution of the population and eliminating underdeveloped areas. At this point my pilgrims started snickering. It seemed to me, however, that of all freedoms the easiest to sacrifice would be the freedom to starve.

Noiret, our mini-Napoleon, asked about the attitude of Mao's government toward birth control. Pariet said that a huge birth control campaign had been launched during the "Hundred Flowers" period in 1956, when Mao had tried to introduce freedom of speech, freedom of thought, and freedom of the press and to encourage constructive criticism. Even though it had been backed by lectures given by doctors and nurses in both town and country, the campaign had been an almost total failure. The illiterate masses had been unwilling to change their ancient customs. To avoid losing face completely, the government had given up birth control and announced that China needed all its children to repopu-

75

late its western provinces and that man was the only effective weapon against the nuclear weapons of the imperialists. This had ended the Hundred Flowers period and the accompanying wave of vitriolic criticism, which in its violence had endangered the very existence of the regime. Mao had altered course, and China had become a caldron of autocriticism, arrests, trials, disappearances, and re-education in distant communes.

Since the meeting between Khrushchev and Eisenhower at Camp David in 1959, China had worked out a new political philosophy: as Russian collusion with American imperialism left China isolated, the country could survive only by the overwhelming number of its inhabitants. Or as Mao had declared: "Even if the United States kills four hundred million Chinese with its atom bombs, three hundred million will be left to rebuild the country." The fact remained that while it was waiting for the atom bombs to be dropped, China had to feed seven hundred million mouths three hundred and sixty-five days a year. That was why, as Shu had explained to me, the regime "recommended" that the Chinese not marry before twenty-five in the case of women and thirty in the case of men. Abortion was allowed for families that already had three children. Mao advised the Chinese not to have more than two children and urged sterilization on the parents of large families.

Listening to these explanations, the Italian women in the group uttered little cries of disgust while the French women remained silent. The men all looked horrified, confusing fecundity and virility in a common Mediterranean reaction.

Outside, cultivated fields appeared less often. The earth was brown, bare, and occasionally cracked. Walls curved like giant shinbones protected trees that looked like skeletons in the brief dusk.

About half past ten at night we arrived at Loyang. It had taken us fourteen and a half hours to cover just over four hundred miles. On the whole the journey had been pleasant, with the sweet charm of observing an enclosed, *fin-de-siècle* world in which life goes on against a slowly changing background. On the platform Shin introduced us to three men in gabardine coats, who led us courteously to a bus. The foyer of the hotel was rather shabby, with a cement floor and peeling white walls; but the rooms were quite pleasant and the staff, smiling. At dawn the next day, jumping into a rough stone bathtub, I thought how lucky we were to see Loyang. Very few foreigners have been allowed to visit this ancient little walled town that

Mao has turned into one of the biggest industrial centers in the country. In less than fifteen years the population of Loyang has risen from fifty thousand to six hundred thousand. I was happy to feel that at last we had reached the inaccessible, closely guarded, mysterious China I had dreamed about since childhood.

Yuan and I had worked out the program the night before, sitting on wooden chairs under a blinking light bulb that hung from the ceiling of the bleak hotel foyer. In the dining room at breakfast, Laure chatted with a wrinkled waiter who told us in French that he was fifty years old. It was amusing to hear a Chinese who was neither a teacher nor an interpreter speaking very lively, almost slangy French. He had been a steward on a French steamer for several years and was obviously delighted to be able to tell us his life story, for he burst out laughing after every sentence. But when two other waiters arrived he made a slight bow and walked away smiling.

Colette and Mme. Chapeau were missing at breakfast. I found them still in bed, flu-ridden, feverish, and pale, and I comforted them as best I could with aspirins and kind words.

Our destination that day was the Lungmen caves, one of the great sanctuaries of Chinese art, which had been closed to foreigners since the revolution. On the way our bus drove through modern Loyang, which had broad tree-lined avenues, three-storied concrete houses, parks full of flowers, and big shopping centers. There were a great many cyclists on the road, for it was nearly time for the offices and shops to open. Then we found ourselves out in the country, golden and beautiful in the morning sunshine. Maize fields were followed by cornfields dotted with colorful pyramids of ripe melons. A few peasants were already at work, generally in groups of six, and the road was crowded with hundreds of carts drawn by donkeys, men, or women. Sometimes these carts carried children, sometimes a solitary old man jolting up and down with every pothole; but more often the carts were laden with big oval baskets full of rags, coal dust, or maize. Shu proudly pointed out that these humble vehicles nearly always had rubber tires, "which produce a reduction in friction and noise."

I was constantly reminded how obsessive the Chinese are about noise and dirt and how stubbornly they are trying to annihilate them both. The accounts of travelers who knew the old China frequently mention the shouting and excrement, the stench of the towns, and the filthiness of the villages. Present-day China, on the other hand, seems to be inhabited by people who talk only in measured tones—except for the announcers whose voices, generously amplified by loud-speakers, scatter to the four winds the praises of Chairman Mao and of the civic virtues, notably silence. Because nearly all farm produce is transported in small carts, there can be no doubt that the use of rubber tires has reduced the noise in both town and country. Another remarkable postrevolutionary improvement is the elimination of the fly. That minor scourge of ancient China has now almost entirely vanished. I saw only one fly during the journey—in Nanking—and then I politely pretended not to have seen it. During the first few years of the new regime it was the civic duty of every good Chinese to kill at least six flies a day!

After an hour's drive the bus crossed the Lo River, a lazy yellow stream that winds through gentle hilly country. On its banks I caught sight of my first tractor, which Shin swore was Chinese-made.

Lungmen is Buddha's China. Carved into the walls of stone grottoes is a fantastic gallery of more than three thousand sculptures constituting one of the marvels of Chinese art. Looking up, I faced a serenely ironic Buddha flanked by grimacing guardians and groups of miniature Buddhas cut out of the gray-gold rock. A huge cliff covered with rank weeds and wildflowers serves as a roof and shelter for this fantastic creation begun by the Weis in the fifth and sixth centuries A.D. We followed Pariet along the right bank of the river into the first grottoes, where we could just make out in the shadowy background the traditional group of Buddha and his guardians. These, the oldest of the Lungmen sculptures, were carved in the Han period, from the second century B.C. to the third century A.D., which was to Chinese art what Greco-Roman civilization was to Western art. The carving was massive and vigorous, and the faces were impressive despite a certain fixity of expression. My pilgrims were spellbound—especially Torti, who made ecstatic clucking noises. Only Pariet seemed unaffected and muttered a few grumpy commonplaces.

"For God's sake," I said to him at the third grotto, "let's have a bit of lyricism! Say anything that comes into your head—give us a description, a commentary, a few anecdotes."

With a deepening scowl, he answered, "I can't help it. I haven't got an artistic mind." There we were at the heart of China, with a dear little expert who hadn't an artistic mind. Behind me Boilèle complained, for once with some justification, "That idiot doesn't know a thing! It's a swindle!" The others too, even the nice ones, started grumbling. "He's rather dry, your little pal," said Noiret, and I could only sympathize. I could have strangled Pariet and myself as well.

In the Grotto of the Thousand Buddhas I tried to the best of my limited ability to remedy the deficiencies of our "cultural adviser." This delicately harmonious grotto

80

is completely lined with statuettes of smiling Buddhas carved out of the rock. The T'ang grottoes that followed were so much admired that to my relief they all forgot Pariet in their fascination with the flowing draperies and fuller faces that foreshadowed Indo-Aryan art. I chattered on rather shamefacedly, and except for Torti everybody listened kindly. The last accessible grotto was partly hidden under the cliff and had partly fallen in. As we emerged, it was pleasant to feel the gentle sun and to breathe the spicy air. The river glistened like brown satin, and the elegant arch of the modern bridge was silhouetted against the gilded landscape. Our party split up. We had half an hour before lunch, so I returned to my favorite grottoes for a last visit. In one I found Georges Wolf and Dupont, in another, Laure, and then nobody. As I walked slowly back toward the restaurant, lingering on a delicate little arched bridge made of carved white stone, I noticed Adrienne Mandois sitting in the back of the bus. She must be ill again, I thought, and I rushed over to find out what was wrong.

"Why, no, my dear," she murmured, "I'm perfectly all right. But what do you expect me to do in your grottoes? In any case, I'd have forgotten everything in ten minutes!"

I nearly choked at the thought of certain friends of mine who would have given a great deal to be there. They would not be sitting in the back of a bus, nor would they pontificate about China at society dinner tables during the following season.

The great Buddha looked utterly placid. I sat down at the entrance to one of the grottoes and once again felt calmed by the cool serenity and unchanging peace of the place.

On the terrace of the restaurant my so-called art lovers were laughing and drinking beer. They had already forgotten their few precious hours in this unique spot to which they would never return.

Still, I could offer a silent hymn of praise for Chinese beer after seeing the effect it had on Pariet. At last he started giving a few dates and telling an occasional anecdote. My companions too were more relaxed. The river turned pink, and I sensed that everyone, even Yuan, was overcome by the idyllic calm of the scene. When I asked him for permission to go for a walk in the old section of Loyang before returning to the hotel, he agreed at once.

On the way to Loyang the bus stopped outside a majestic wooden temple, now a museum of Neolithic tools and pottery. The exhibits were in very good condition and were well displayed. While our party was inspecting the collection with every sign of interest, a voice suddenly reached us from the bottom of the garden. It was Boilèle shouting, "We're wasting our time here! No, I refuse to budge an inch to go and see a lot of old pots!"

The outburst disgusted Pariet, who emerged from a stubborn silence only for a few exchanges with the Chinese. Luckily our next stop, another temple, brought a smile of genuine happiness to the old general's lips. Torti too became ecstatic over the enormous and priceless collection of T'ang pottery, the dozens of statuettes of dancers, favorites, cameleers with or without camels, and horses with or without riders, all in glass cases dark with dust and insect droppings (though not, I need scarcely say, fly droppings). Boilèle had a few specimens of this period in his own collection, and his delight brought him to the verge of tears. But just as I was beginning to think he was not such a bad fellow after all, I heard him thundering at Shin: "It's an absolute scandal displaying treasures like these so badly! In a European museum, every one of these wonderful pieces would be exhibited in a separate showcase and not left in this dusty pile."

I froze as Shin translated this masterpiece of diplomacy for Yuan's benefit. Yuan said nothing, but his smile vanished as if it had been wiped off his face. Shin looked embarrassed. Dear, subtle Laure saved the situation by suggesting maliciously, "European museums couldn't leave their rare Chinese pieces in a pile even if they wanted to, because they haven't got enough to make a pile of."

This was exactly the thing to say, since the Chinese consider that works of art from their country now in foreign museums have been stolen from them.

The fields were being worked by wooden plows drawn by odd teams consisting of a horse and a donkey, an ox and a horse, or a donkey and an ox. There were not enough draft animals, Shin explained, to provide matched teams. The countryside was full of little groups of peasants stooping over their scythes. We stopped for a moment beside a cotton field, a vast brown expanse studded with white flowers being picked by women and children. We took pictures of a mother and her ten-year-old son, who were gazing at us inquisitively. Signora Negri remarked in her shrill voice, "Shin, I thought that child labor had been abolished and that all Chinese children went to school."

"That is correct," Shin replied imperturbably, "but nobody can prevent a child from helping his mother after he comes home from school."

A little farther on I noticed a couple of ancient tractors in a cornfield. China imported and manufactured tractors, Pariet explained, in order to free labor for work in regions that were still undeveloped.

"But we are still very short of motorized transport,"

Shin broke in, anticipating the sneers of the Boilèle-Mandois group.

On the road we overtook long lines of carts pulled by tired, bent, hollow-faced men. As we walked through the old section of Loyang, a crowd followed us. They wanted nothing more than to smile at us; in the eyes of these men and women living in the heart of China, our presence in their country meant that we could only be friends of the Chinese people. Somebody in our group clapped his hands and soon we were surrounded by a circle of loud applause, which went on until we got back into the bus. Three girls asked me where I came from.

"*Faguo*" ("France"), I replied.

They looked blank. It was obvious that the name meant nothing to them.

"They are only country girls," said Shin apologetically.

Suddenly they burst out laughing, pointing, as usual, to my shoes and stockings. Feeling like a reigning monarch, I slowly walked along the narrow streets lined with little houses of brick or mud roofed with gray tile. Through open doors I glimpsed long narrow rooms, humble but clean, in which men in singlets and women in light smocks were gossiping and drinking tea around rickety old tables. Squatting in front of one door, a couple of old men were playing cards on the beaten earth. Some of the old women—dressed in black, their feet bound, and their hair done in tight little chignons—were holding small children by the hand.

The many street stalls sold mainly vegetables, fruit, or rice. A cooper was hammering lustily at a metal bar. His neighbor the coppersmith was working in the narrow corridor of his house. Farther on, as in Peking, a cobbler was cutting sandals out of old tires. Both yards and streets were very clean, and the children were round, pink, healthy, and well fed. The clothes people wore were

84

often patched with material of different colors, but they were all clean. Only one very old man with a long white beard ambled along in tatters, looking pitifully haggard. As we turned a corner into a narrow alley, an ecstatic Pariet dragged me into a big, dark bookshop lined with shelves sagging under the weight of thousands of volumes and presided over, of course, by a portrait of Mao. Pariet was looking for a geography book. A smiling sales-girl with a pigtail informed him that she was not allowed to sell him any books. Pariet smiled back and asked in Chinese, "Why not? Do you take me for a spy? Even if I *were* a spy, don't you think that with their satellites the Americans have already photographed everything that interests them about the geography of China?"

The girl burst out laughing and immediately brought him three dusty volumes, which he accepted reverentially, promising, as she had requested, that nobody would know anything about it.

The bus was waiting for us in a little square packed with people. Noiret started the clapping game again. The crowd followed his lead, clapping frantically and smiling. Suddenly Pariet's enthusiasm kindled, and with an eloquence I had unfortunately never encountered in him before, he began to speak in Chinese. The predominantly young onlookers applauded every sentence, almost splitting their sides with laughter. Watching Pariet, I reflected on the magic power of language to break through frontiers and into hearts.

The rear guard of our party, with its milling escort, gradually caught up with us. Adrienne Mandois was simpering, smiling, and waving her gloved hand, uncertain whether to imitate Chairman Mao or the queen of England. It was the first time since I had arrived in China that I had had the impression of living in a human ant heap.

My pilgrims set off in the radiant, scented morning air toward two very different destinations. Pariet's group was going to visit the second largest ball-bearing factory in China. I was taking my little party to a school.

We walked single file across a pretty little courtyard planted with flowers and trees, where we were greeted by a young headmistress with a warm smile, a low voice, and a barber's bowl hairdo. In a white room that opened on the garden we assembled for the traditional preliminary conference and pale-green tea. As usual Chairman Mao surveyed us from the wall. The headmistress was all buttoned up in a black suit, and her finely chiseled features made her seem both intelligent and likeable. It was terribly frustrating to be unable to understand what she was saying, the more so because Shu's monolithic mind obviously failed to appreciate the nuances. Translated into inadequate French, the headmistress' remarks reached us only as a litany of basic facts and figures. We were in Tsing-Tse school, which had 52 teachers and employees and 1,330 pupils, 95 per cent of whom were the children of workers and peasants. The school covered an area of 1,000 square yards compared with 550 square yards in 1947, when it had had only 270 pupils, nearly all of them from landowning families and the upper middle class. We were asked to remember Chairman Mao's words: "Education must be used for the benefit of the people and combined with manual labor to rid the minds of the intellectuals of any idea of class superiority."

In 1958 the school had set up some small workshops where the children could go after their lessons and do what they liked. The ladies in my party were very attentive, except Adrienne Mandois, who gave a huge yawn that aired every one of her crown fillings.

Since the liberation, the headmistress doggedly continued, 3,311 pupils had left the school with a primary school certificate. The best of them had gone on to secondary schools, and the rest had gone to work in the fields and factories, where some of them had become "star workers." Comrade Hu-Sin-Shua, for example, had been a very lazy pupil full of evil instincts. She had hated manual labor and had had a lively penchant for private ownership. Now she was one of the star workers in the town: she had become an excellent waitress.

"A waitress!" sneered the incorrigible Mme. Mandois. "That's nothing to boast about."

I must confess that I found the little story rather naive, but I was deeply touched by this headmistress who had given meaning to her life by helping to rescue three thousand children from ignorance.

Dupont's Geneva accent made me smile again as he broke in with assumed bonhomie, "Oh, being a waitress isn't so bad. Twenty years ago her starving parents would probably have sold her to the first comer at the roadside."

The tour of the school began. In the music room a graceful young woman with long braids and gentle features sat at a little old piano playing what sounded like a harpsichord melody. She sang in a sweet voice, and a score of little dolls with pink cheeks and red smocks repeated the refrain while flapping their arms to imitate the flight of a butterfly.

Next we came to a large radio workshop where about thirty ten-year-olds were sitting around a long table. Each child was working with intense concentration on his own little transistor radio, performing delicate soldering operations by dipping tiny tools into a pot containing molten metal. Unlike schools in France, where visitors are usually greeted with noisy, giggling curiosity, here you could have heard a pin drop.

In the paint shop the boys were sandpapering little wooden boxes, which the girls painted red and then varnished. These boxes would house the transistor radios being assembled in the next room. Again there was complete silence; not a single child looked up. It was almost intimidating.

The same concentration was apparent in the scale-model workshop, except for a little girl with skin as downy as an apricot who was having trouble with the wings of her model aircraft. She heaved a noisy sigh of exasperation and she had the same expression—half sad, half angry—that I had often seen on my daughter's face when she was having trouble with a difficult Latin translation. This outburst of anger in the midst of those well-trained little robots first amused and relieved me, then rather worried me. Devotion to the collective good was incompatible with impatience and independence. I foresaw many difficult hours of autocriticism for my unknown little friend.

The most astonishing course at the school was the Morse code class. While a young teacher dictated, the room resounded with the clicking of his pupils' transmitters. Every Chinese child, the headmistress explained, had to be able to take part in the defense of his country in the event of an attack. At the first warning, a Morse code intelligence network would promptly blanket China.

At the kindergarten my ladies were surprised and delighted by the white rooms furnished with little beds and low tables of pale wood. The chubby, red-cheeked infants, their dark eyes flashing like sparks, sang for us in piping voices what my companions called charming, adorable songs. They were in fact hymns praising Uncle Mao and calling down destruction upon the capitalist invaders.

Mme. Mandois, in an admirable show of motherly affection, swooped down on a tiny little boy, lifted him off his feet, and pressed him to her bosom. Although courtesy and self-control are national virtues in China, I don't think I have ever heard so tiny a boy howl so loudly. Shin, Isabella, and I nearly split our sides laughing. The terror of the poor infant as he saw that huge scarlet mouth approaching must have been the more overwhelming because people so rarely kiss in China—never in public, certainly; possibly in private, but in any case not at the drop of a hat as they do in France.

The smiling headmistress led us back to the conference room, where she invited our questions about the school.

"What proportion of the national budget is devoted to education?" Pierre Adjouf asked.

The headmistress replied, "The government gives what is necessary."

"Is education compulsory?" asked Dr. Blum. "And if so, are there enough schools?"

The young woman replied that since the liberation the number of schools had grown rapidly. Now over 95 per cent of the country's children went to school.

One of the Italian women wanted to know how many years a child spent at school before going to a university.

"From seven to fourteen, children go to primary school," replied the headmistress, "then to secondary school until the age of twenty. After that they have a chance of entering a university."

Back at the hotel I found Colette Quesnel feeling feverish and depressed. Shu and I appealed to the hotel manager, a calm, courteous man with a trim figure (the traditional "fat Chinese" was obviously a thing of the past). He immediately telephoned for a doctor and had tea served. Five minutes later the doctor arrived, a man of about forty with steel-rimmed spectacles and a fawn gabardine suit. Like the hotel manager he spoke only Chinese. This meant that he had been trained entirely in China; most doctors over forty had studied in the United States or Europe. I took him to see his patient. Expecting to be examined, she pushed away the bed-clothes, which she had pulled right up to her nose. To our surprise, the doctor stopped her with a gesture, stood in the doorway of the room, and put his hand to his own throat and coughed, at the same time raising his eyebrows in mute inquiry. Colette nodded, brandishing the thermometer with one hand while indicating with the other that she had a very high temperature. The strange long-distance examination was over, and still at the doorway, the doctor wrote out a very pretty prescription in Chinese characters and handed it to Shu. Then he bowed in the direction of his patient without so much as looking at her and disappeared. Shu seemed surprised at our bewilderment. She explained that no Chinese doctor would ever take the liberty of examining a woman. This fact explained the charming ivory statuettes representing a naked woman, which were known as doctors' women. Sick women used to indicate on the statuette where they felt pain. We had seen several of these figurines in antique shops, some of them quite old and beautifully carved.

Colette was considerably cheered by the remote-control diagnosis, and Shu and I set off in search of a drugstore. After wandering along busy little streets all splashed with sunshine, we came to a cool, dark pharmacy at the corner of a wide avenue. In exchange for the pretty prescription, two pale, sour-looking men reluctantly gave us a tube of tiny white pills. I asked for three more tubes, foreseeing a possible deterioration in the health of our little group. The walls of the shop were lined with oak shelves filled with colored glass jars, as in old-fashioned English pharmacies. I started rummaging around on the shelves as if I were in an antique shop, which did not at all please the two clerks.

On my return to the hotel I discovered that Laure too was sniffling, shivering, and coughing. Mme. Chapeau was still in bed and looked very pale. The prospects for the rest of the journey looked decidedly poor. What was worse, my nicest companions had fallen ill, as if laid low by some spiteful Chinese germ.

I took the survivors to visit the Temple of the White Horse, dedicated to the monk Hsüan Tsang, who in the seventh century, under the T'ang dynasty, had traveled to India and brought back the writings of Buddha. He had returned on a white horse and had died as soon as he arrived home. Noiret asked if we could see the statue of the white horse, for he had read somewhere that one existed.

"Yes, where is the white horse?" repeated Signora Leandri.

"The white horse?" I said. "I haven't the faintest idea. Shin, where is the white horse?"

Shin followed my example and swiftly passed the buck: "The white horse? I don't know. Monsieur Pariet, where is the white horse?"

"There is no statue of the white horse," declared Pariet triumphantly. "It disappeared during one of your many civil wars."

Some people always manage to carry off bluffs like that, but not Pariet. Two days later we found the statue of the white horse in the Sian museum.

As we drove on, fields speckled with snowy flakes of cotton stretched away to the foot of distant blue hills. Standing on a horse-drawn wooden harrow, a huge man appeared for a moment. Stripped to the waist, with bulging muscles and a shaven head, he drove his horse as if he were in a chariot race. This centaur looked as if he had descended from some Oriental Olympus and loomed strangely large in this nation of ants. In an instant he was gone, and I shall never know how that man from another race had ended up in China. Wherever we looked there were the same wooden plows drawn by half a dozen men; the same haggard, stooping peasants with vacant eyes, dragging the same carts piled high with cotton and bricks; the same women bent double, picking cotton in groups of twenty; the same busy crowds and heavy traffic. Cyclists came so close that they almost rode under the wheels of our bus, which was proceeding at a terrifying speed while the horn blared insistently. The egotism of human nature is irrepressible, Mao and his teachings notwithstanding.

92

Our next stop was a public park ablaze with flowers where two Han tombs had been reconstructed. They had been recently discovered some distance away by workmen digging the foundations for a new railway line. To the delight of archaeologists, almost every time a bridge, a dam, a railway, or an apartment house is built, the pickaxe of a Chinese laborer turns up a bronze, a shard of ancient pottery, or a statue. When that happens the local archaeological service immediately assesses the importance of the find. The government has encouraged the formation of excellent teams of young archaeologists trained by scholars educated in American or European universities. Pariet told us that these teams had made extraordinary finds, some of which were on display in the Sian museum, that had rendered a few excellent studies on Chinese art inadequate or out-of-date. Unfortunately the Chinese publish only very incomplete reports about their excavations. When I expressed astonishment that tombs should have been moved from their original locations, Shin said that it was "easier for the people'to come and see them in a public park than beside a railway track." I saw his point. The park, like all Chinese gardens, was delightful. The air was heavy with the scent of magnolia and wisteria, and hydrangeas bloomed in balls of red, white, or blue. A little wooden bridge arched gracefully over a slow-moving river that reflected a weeping willow.

We were strolling happily in the peace of the gathering dusk when Georges Wolf suddenly seized my hand and slipped into my palm a tiny piece of Han carving that he had found on the ground. I was delighted and felt no remorse whatever at becoming a grave robber.

My patients were still in a bad way. Laure, however, promised to get up to attend the dinner that the government delegation to Loyang was giving in our honor. The head of the delegation was a woman in her forties, dressed in the obligatory pantsuit, this time of dark gray gabardine. But her short hair, round face, beautiful, firm features, and dazzling smile charmed us immediately. She and I sat down beside each other, but once again, alas, the wretched language barrier confined us to talking about the Parisian climate and Chinese cooking. The indispensable interpreter proved an insuperable obstacle to any remotely personal conversation.

At the beginning of the dinner the lady delegate delivered a speech on the usual themes: the friendship between our two peoples, and the hope that we had enjoyed our stay in Loyang—a very old city and now a great industrial center, which was proud of its important tractor factory. Would we, she asked, care to "correct their deficiencies"? The request was familiar, but this woman struck me as being genuinely moved and thus very moving. I thanked her and to my own surprise launched into a lyrical little speech, likewise full of sincere emotion, in which I assured her of our interest, our friendship, and our admiration for all that they had achieved. Because we knew the state of corruption and poverty that had existed before, we were amazed that China had been able to improve the lot of her people in so short a time and that the problems of food, housing, education, and economic development were being so rapidly solved without outside help. No doubt there still remained a long way to go, but we all hoped that this people we had begun to love would reach the end of that road without too much suffering. To my embarrassment, my companions burst into applause. Our hostess stood up and frantically shook both my hands. Shin murmured, "Thank you, madame, thank you." Yuan came over, looked me in the eye, said *"Kampei,"* and we drained our glasses at a gulp.

94

Fifteen exquisite dishes were served one after another by an army of mute waiters. We had all become accustomed to handling chopsticks and we served ourselves straight from the dish. The little glasses of warm brownish wine followed in quick succession. Voices became louder and cheeks grew flushed. Laure stood up and made a charming little speech thanking the Chinese, Pariet, and me. Noiret, who by now was as drunk as a lord, made subtle references to Marco Polo's visiting Kublai Khan laden with gifts, whereas we had nothing to offer but our friendship. I privately doubted whether our hosts even knew Kublai Khan's name. Then, to my alarm, Torti got to his feet, made some involved remarks about the renaissance of modern China, and expressed the hope that the country would not go too far. Adrienne Mandois then showed every intention of making her own little speech. Fearing the worst, I brought the dinner to an abrupt end before Shin had even translated Torti's remarks. Fortunately the bowl of rice we could not touch was already on the table. The Chinese never linger when their banquets are over, thank God.

At eight o'clock in the morning on the platform of Loyang station Colette and Laure were pale and ill, Mme. Chapeau was shaken by fits of coughing, Mme. Blum was depressed, and Georges Wolf was swathed in cashmere shawls like a mummy. Only the Italians were still in good shape.

"It's all the *mao-tai* I keep drinking that protects me against the Siberian virus," Signora Leandri explained.

Something remote and exotic like a Siberian virus, of course, had to be responsible for everything, down to the pimple on Noiret's nose. All the same, morale was not too bad, the day was warm and sunny, and the train, clean and comfortable. We settled down, four to a compartment, for the twenty-six-hour ride to Sian. To my delight, Colette, Laure, and Señora Neralinda invited me to share their compartment and their germs. We traveled past more loess hills, a landscape that would linger in my mind as one of the most characteristic in China. All four of us snuggled down under the soft floral eiderdowns and went to sleep. In the other compartments the Italians were playing cards, the Blums and the Adjoufs were chatting, Mme. Chapeau was knitting, and the rest were reading. Toward the end of the morning the Musketeers came to keep us company; they sat on the lower bunks and told us about their sentimental experiences. We drank pints of tea as the loess hills glided past our jolting car like frames in a slow-motion film.

At one o'clock in the afternoon I led my party to the diner through eight cars, each with its washbasin and spittoon and the traditional hierarchy of wooden benches, hard seats, and upholstered bunks with lace antimacassars. Every compartment was packed with people. Young men, soldiers, and whole families were sleeping, talking or playing cards while mothers were nursing their babies.

In the dining car Colette and I faced Adrienne Mandois and Shin. Adrienne treated us to a series of jokes in doubtful taste about Shin's probable sexual abilities. Shin pretended not to hear, and we showed our disapproval by saying nothing. Finally Colette lost patience and advised Adrienne to tackle Shin directly. To our horror she promptly asked, "Shin, have you ever been to bed with a woman?"

"No," replied the crimson-faced Shin.

"How old are you?"

"Twenty-nine."

"Then why haven't you slept with a woman?"

Shin was still blushing but he replied in a firm voice,

"Because that sort of thing isn't done in China any more when you aren't married. It was all right in the corrupt days of the previous regime."

"You don't mean to tell me," said Adrienne, "that Chinese bachelors never make love?"

"Never. We are allowed to marry at thirty, and girls at twenty-five."

"And what happens," Adrienne asked, "to the exception, to the man who makes love even though he's a bachelor?"

"He is reprimanded. He has to make his autocriticism and marry the girl."

Adrienne persisted, "And what if he refuses to marry her?"

"Then that proves that he is not sufficiently familiar with the thoughts of Chairman Mao and needs re-educating."

"Where?" asked Adrienne.

"Usually in an agricultural commune."

I intervened. "Do you know a girl now, Shin, whom you would like to marry?"

Blushing furiously again—for in China personal questions are considered indiscreet, not friendly—Shin replied, "No, I haven't met such a girl yet."

"What sort of girl do you think you would like to marry?" I asked. "Would you like her to be pretty, intellectual, or what?"

"If she's pretty, so much the better, but above all she must be virtuous."

Colette asked, "Which virtue strikes you as the most precious of all: honesty, charity, kindness, or what?"

Shin replied crisply—and inevitably, "The thoughts of Chairman Mao."

With some irritation I said, "Shin, that's going too far. Chairman Mao is a very great man. Nobody can deny that. But though his thoughts are the fruits of a mind of genius, they surely can't be classed as virtues, can they?"

"You are right, madame," came the reply, "I express myself badly in French." (Autocriticism again.) "What I meant was the virtue that leads us to follow the thoughts of Chairman Mao."

I was appalled to see that he was sincere, even fervent. How could a decent, intelligent man like Shin sink into such fanatical obscurantism? No doubt this leveling of human thought was necessary to lift seven hundred million people out of the mud. The life of the mind was regarded as a luxury that could wait until material security had been assured for everyone. But for the moment I was talking not to seven hundred million Chinese, but to my good friend Shin, and it was a painful experience.

"What would you like to do later on?" I asked him.

"I shall probably be a diplomat."

"Is that what you want to be?"

"Yes, because that is the field in which I think I can best serve the people."

"What career would you have chosen if you had followed your own inclination?"

Shin hesitated before answering. "I would have liked to be an engineer."

"Don't you regret having given up a scientific career?"

"No," he said, "because I am more useful to my country in other ways."

"What does your father do?" I asked.

"Before the liberation he was a diplomat. At present he is a professor at the School of Diplomatic Science in Peking."

This fact accounted for Shin's physical distinction, his long hands, and his good manners. His father, doubtless a member of the upper middle class, had probably welcomed the new regime hopefully, like many liberals and intellectuals disillusioned by the crimes and misery of the previous period. He had probably been asked to write a complete and sincere history of himself and his family, a sort of genealogical autocriticism quite in keeping with the Chinese tradition of recording for future generations the life stories of the remotest relatives. After having been carefully studied, his account had presumably been accepted, his faults had been judged venial, and he had been declared recoverable for the purpose of training new cadres. Thanks to this system, revolutionary China did not suffer that chaotic intermediate period without highly trained personnel that has crippled the development of many young nations. So long as they were not guilty of crimes against the people, so long as they were innocent of murder, looting, and oppression, many leading members of the upper middle class were "recovered" in this way. So were many guilty men: a few former warlords now occupy seats in the National Assembly. China has not hesitated to retain certain factory owners as managers, and to use the services of such scientists and doctors with bourgeois origins as Dr. Wong, until the new generation born of the people can take their place.

The railway line now ran between high plateaus covered with sparse undergrowth. Cultivated fields and trees became more numerous. As we approached Sian, sundown reddened the horizon, which swiftly vanished into a golden mist.

13

Sian, which for many centuries was the capital of China and is now the capital of Shensi Province, was the terminal point of the Long March. The little mountain town of Yenan served as the headquarters of the Red Army. Consequently Shensi Province soon became the proving ground for Maoism and later the "new frontier" of the new China. In that remote province Sian is a mysterious town barred to nearly all foreign travelers. Only a few writers such as Edgar Snow, who devotes a chapter to it in his book *The Other Side of the River,* have visited Sian since the revolution. I had no idea why we had been allowed to come.

I felt that we were incredibly lucky to be treading the

pale-blue carpet and sitting in the comfortable armchairs of the pretty red pagoda that is the Sian station. After meeting the three local representatives of Luxingsche, we scrambled aboard a Hungarian bus like schoolchildren and soon we were driving along narrow streets with small gray houses reminiscent of Loyang. But in this provincial capital the roofs were covered with shining yellow tiles and the ridges were turned up and decorated with delicate statues of dragons, horsemen, soldiers, and lions. We passed the superb red and gold columns of Ming belfries and splendidly restored Ming ramparts with four towers, which protected the old town. The modern city of broad avenues, three-storied or four-storied apartment buildings, shopping centers, and factories was built outside the ancient walls.

Adrienne yawned. "You don't get enough vitamins in this damned country," she groaned, lamenting the lack of apples.

The bus stopped in the old town, and we were immediately surrounded by a smiling crowd. Pariet, who was now used to being a curiosity, trotted out a pretty little speech in Chinese that drew roars of laughter and applause. But Shin cut short our exhilarating popular success by dragging us off to our hotel. A few grumbles were heard on the way.

"What sort of dump are we going to find in a town where there are never any tourists?" asked Signora Leandri, who was beginning to find China "a little prrrimitive."

In fact, the hotel was a large modern building put up in the fifties to accommodate Russian technicians and their families. Each bedroom had an adjoining sitting room with deep armchairs, writing paper, and the inevitable thermos of hot water and canister of green tea. The bathroom had the familiar tarlike smell of the rather

102

rough pink soap provided by Chinese hotels. The service was excellent; the luggage was delivered in no time at all, and for once everybody seemed delighted.

Yuan, Shin, Shu, and I held our ritual conference with the three local tourist agents to review the program they had drawn up. We drank tea and I handed around American cigarettes. I praised the achievements of the People's Government, spoke warmly of the friendship with which we were always greeted, and stressed our long-time fascination with Sian. I therefore counted on our hosts' boundless understanding to allow us one minor change in the program: a visit to a temple instead of a factory. I explained that there were some art lovers in our party who would be delighted by such a favor. I also said that our common aim remained the success of the tour for the greater benefit of the community. I had become very "Chinese." I never spoke of "individuals" now, but always of the "community." Shin translated my speech with genuine sympathy and seemed to support what I had said by the tone of his voice. The local agents consulted among themselves and finally agreed to my request. I thanked them effusively and after countless handshakes I went off to wash my lingerie, mend the hem of my only skirt, resew the buttons on my one, shapeless jacket, and finally sink into a hot bath.

The dining room looked like the restaurant of a grand hotel with its big round tables and immaculate table-cloths. Hardly had we sat down when Boilèle started complaining about the delicious food; he was copied immediately by the other grumblers. This decided me to institute two tables: a "European table" and a "Chinese table." I lost no time in fleeing the steak-and-french-fries brigade forever. Indeed, all the friendly members of the party, all those who were prepared to contribute more to the journey than a suitcase, joined the Chinese table.

103

The next morning I awoke about seven as a ray of sunshine filtered between the heavy brown velvet curtains. My room overlooked a huge square of beaten earth. In the middle the ground was marked with concentric white circles, and young men in track suits were running between the lines. The square was dotted with little figures doing slow calisthenics punctuated by the whistle blasts that had disturbed my last hour of sleep. On the right was a huge circus tent, and I resolved to try to change our planned evening at the opera for an evening at the circus.

That day we were to visit the T'ang tombs, about forty miles outside Sian, and see the famous frescoes depicting the unfortunate Empress Wu Tai. That luckless lady had run afoul of a cruel concubine, the emperor's favorite, who persuaded the emperor to chop off Wu Tai's hands and feet. The frescoes depict the empress' daily life and are a unique example of eighth-century Chinese painting. This visit to the T'ang tombs was to be one of the high spots of the tour, and the curator of the Cernuschi Museum in Paris had asked Laure and me to photograph them, for there were no pictures of either tombs or frescoes in existence.

I had naturally taken care to confirm the excursion as soon as we arrived. Hence the violent cramp that twisted my long-suffering stomach when I saw Shin's expression.

"We are terribly sorry, Madame Modiano," he said, "but we shall not be able to visit the T'ang tombs this morning."

Tense with suppressed fury, I asked, "Then when shall we be able to visit them, my dear Shin?"

"Never, I'm afraid," he answered sheepishly.

"And why not, if I may ask?"

"The road is very bad. There has been a lot of rain recently."

104

"Was the road any better last night," I asked, "when we worked out our program together?"

"I'm afraid not," said Shin. "In any case, it's very bad today."

"Is there any chance it might be better tomorrow," I inquired, "if the rain stops?"

"I don't think so," he replied firmly. "There are workers resurfacing the road."

"We don't mind an uncomfortable journey," I pointed out, "provided we see the frescoes."

"We are terribly sorry, Madame Modiano, but we simply can't go there. The road is very bad and we cannot possibly take you along bad roads."

And that was that. I sighed with exasperation. Shin sighed with embarrassment. We looked at each other, and I smiled wanly. Neither of us could do a thing to change the situation.

My little party was wrapped in raincoats and bristling with umbrellas like a giant porcupine. The reception they gave my bad news was as cool as the weather.

Laure exclaimed, "My dear, that's impossible. You've simply got to *do* something."

Colette grumbled between fits of coughing, "Are you sure there's nothing to be done?"

Noiret snarled angrily, "It's disgusting. These people seem quite incapable of honoring their obligations."

M. Chapeau murmured sadly, "What a pity!"

Mme. Adjouf said, "It's very disappointing."

General de Boilèle howled, "It's a scandal! I shall complain to your office in Paris!"

And Mme. Trollan sneered, "I shall demand a refund for part of the tour. This is disgraceful. If you were at all conscientious you would take steps to remedy the situation."

Rather shrilly, I asked my party to get into the bus for

105

a trip to the Shensi Provincial Museum.

It was raining cats and dogs. The beaten earth of Circus Square was a quagmire studded with deep puddles. Nothing could have been more depressing, and there was a sinister silence in the bus as we left the old city.

"I don't suppose we'll see the Pagoda of the Drum either?" snarled Boilèle.

"You are right as usual," I replied. "The Pagoda of the Drum has been taken over to be used as government offices."

Sarcasm didn't help. I looked out glumly at the roofs glistening in the rain and I felt tired—tired of my tourists and of the imperturbable good humor and constant attention they demanded of me; tired of the Chinese and of the endless circumlocutions required for the simplest dealings with them; tired of this strange country that was so fascinating and yet so inaccessible even to foreigners of good will.

I was tired too of trailing around for twelve days in the same suit and especially tired of my untidy hair, which cried for a hairdresser's attention. Hiding behind dark glasses, with a cigarette in my moist, trembling hand, I began to cry.

The grumbling continued behind me. Signora Negri was arguing in her vinegary voice with her daughter, Isabella, who answered that it wasn't my fault and that I probably couldn't do whatever I liked in China. I silently thanked the dear, gay girl.

A bad-tempered busload disembarked at the museum, a former temple of Confucius. It was a succession of graceful red octagonal pagodas with varnished roofs, separated by paved courtyards planted with trees and flowers. Raindrops sparkled on masses of roses; the sun was beginning to shine again, and the general tranquility

106

of the place affected us all. From the tips of the ridge tiles of each pagoda hung little bells that gave a silvery tinkle in the slightest breeze.

Inside the pagoda containing the latest archaeological discoveries was a great hall lighted by frosted glass windows. It was full of huge stone statues: formalized Han Buddhas in their stiff draperies, fourth-century Northern Wei tigers in high relief, and huge Chou bronze vases from the tenth century B.C. I stopped to admire two marble high reliefs of galloping horses from the T'ang tombs to which we had been forbidden access. Beside them stood plaster casts of two motionless horses. Shin whispered to me, "The originals were stolen by the Americans and are now in Philadelphia."

There were whole pagodas filled with Chou vases as big as the bells of Notre Dame; others were crowded with showcases of T'ang pottery camels, cameleers, soldiers, favorites, and dancers. Boilèle was loudly ecstatic: "This is so beautiful I feel like crying!"

The exhibits were interspersed with realistic models showing the peasant revolts of China, so that nobody would forget that the neighboring masterpieces were the result of victories of the people. We then went through the so-called sea of steles, tall slabs of black granite engraved with drawings and historical inscriptions. One of them had been inscribed by the Nestorians—Byzantine Christians who had established themselves in China in the seventh century. Our party was scattered among the various rooms. Some were taking photographs or movies, others were simply admiring a favorite object; everybody was fascinated and happy. The Chinese had disappeared, bored to tears and quite unable to appreciate what Shin called these old things. Indeed, we were the only people in this remarkable and almost unknown museum.

Returning for a last long look at the Wei tiger, I noticed a wooden hut tucked away among the trees. The door was ajar so I peeped inside. Four tall wooden crates leaned against the wall. A little farther on were three more cases that were open. It was rather dark inside the hut and I am nearsighted, so I went in.

There before me were the frescoes from the T'ang tombs! There was Wu Tai, the unlucky empress, still possessed of her hands and feet. Dressed in a long pink gown, with her hair piled high on her head, she was surrounded by her ladies in waiting. Scattered pell-mell on a workbench were T'ang horses and vases that had been found in the same tomb.

I felt like Alice in Wonderland. Alone in that world outside time, I gazed at Wu Tai as if the thirteen centuries that separated us had vanished. This was the explanation of the bad road: because the tombs had been emptied of their treasures there was no longer any reason to visit them. With very little contact between the various departments of the Chinese government, the officials in charge of tourism probably didn't know that the frescoes were in the museum. Possibly they had lied about the road to be polite to their foreign guests and to save face themselves. Westerners, with their passion for unadorned truth, find it difficult to understand the "polite" lies of the Chinese, which nobody is expected to believe. The Chinese wrap their yeses and noes—especially their noes —in more or less plausible stories as a matter of courtesy, just as we wrap our Christmas presents in pretty colored paper. It is difficult to reconcile the two points of view.

I rushed after Shin and hung on his coattails until he begged Yuan to allow my party into the hut. There was a long discussion with the museum officials. Then Shin smiled. "Yes." This, I decided, was my lucky day after all.

108

14

The usual problems awaited my return. Colette was still bronchitic, Mme. Chapeau white-faced, Laure feverish, and Georges Wolf suffering from a cold. Noiret had an eye infection and looked like an albino rabbit, while Adrienne's intestines were still in an uproar. Mme. Blum, who had a bad cold, kept making uncharitable remarks about the rude good health of the Italians.

In the afternoon nobody showed any enthusiasm for the scheduled visit to a textile mill, but I could tell that Yuan was very keen about it and I felt that it would help us negotiate a second visit to the museum.

Flanking the entrance to the mill were large wooden billboards covered with red and yellow posters. These were the "public newspapers."

In the reception room the manager informed us that the mill's 6,000 workers produced 300,000 yards of material a day on 3,200 looms.

Most of the looms in the first workshop were working unattended. The women were dressed in faded cotton trousers, patched but clean, and light-colored blouses, with their hair protected by white scarfs. The men, in overalls or singlets, were sweating in the oppressive heat. We were not spared a single stage in the manufacturing process, from the bales of raw cotton to the final rolls of material.

M. Chapeau remarked, "I've never seen such huge workshops before. And it's all very clean. I gather there are very few looms out of action here. In France there are always more looms out of action—at least four per cent. But one thing surprises me: the absence of any dust extractors."

Most of the workers wore a gauze mask over their nose and mouth; but we were unprotected and we sneezed and spat our way through the mill. On the way M. Chapeau pointed out an English loom, then several Russian looms, and finally a Chinese machine.

On the walls of a corridor between two of the workshops brightly colored posters illustrated the commandments of Mao. They depicted a dear little Chinese with an intelligent face and mischievous eyes, whose actions suggested that his fellow countrymen should wash, work, lead honest lives, exercise daily, go into training to defend China against attack, and most important of all, know by heart the thoughts of Chairman Mao, thanks to which they would be able to follow all the previous recommendations.

At the foot of a staircase leading to the shipping department I found a poster showing the "wicked American," an odious creature with a pale face, a long hooked nose, and red-rimmed eyes (probably due to his indulgence in all the vices). He was being dragged through the mud by magnificent specimens of those peoples that were fighting for their liberty: a Cuban, an African, an Arab, a Vietnamese, and finally someone who looked like the late-lamented Porfirio Rubirosa, probably a Brazilian or a Bolivian. However admirable the objective, this sort of crude hate propaganda is intensely irritating. I recalled the faces of a few American friends and I also remembered the German posters, displayed during their occupation of France, that depicted the Jews as monstrous and ridiculous. Although I stand fairly solidly for freedom and for peace in Vietnam and elsewhere, I felt annoyed. But then I reflected that probably only these crude methods could stir up a huge and largely illiterate population.

When I am thinking, I look either sad or stupid. This time I must have been looking stupid, for the factory guide came up to me and explained, "Americans beaten by world coalition."

Suddenly I felt I had had enough of this humorless officialdom, this dogmatic rule of life, this self-righteous lyricism. I missed the laughter and the irony of France.

Then, walking back through the workshops alone, I was recaptured by my own China and again I felt affection for these smooth-faced women who smiled at me and came to look at my clothes. The men, though more reserved, were moving too. They worked so very hard; they had come so far; they were healthy and well fed, and yet their life was still so precarious. In spite of the occasional irritation of a spoiled liberal, I liked this country I didn't know and these people I couldn't talk to.

At the entrance to the fabric-printing workshop in the next street, the same newspapers were posted on billboards. (In Peking one day I had read an English edition of one of these informational posters. It had contained stories about a visit to the capital by provincial delegations, about a banquet presided over by Chou En-lai, and about the prowess of star worker Tse Tu-tai in swimming across the Yangtze River—no foreign news whatever, unless you counted the departure of a delegation of Chinese workers for Pakistan.)

The manager, a model of urbanity, brought us together for the usual cup of green tea under portraits of Engels, Lenin, Marx, Mao, and six other Chinese whose faces meant nothing to me. He treated us to a long speech, which some of my well-bred companions punctuated with frequent yawns. Lodgings had been provided, he explained, for both families and unmarried workers, as well as a library, sports facilities, schools, nursery schools, kindergartens, and a park.

"Favorable circumstances," he added, "have enabled us to achieve a considerable improvement in the quality of our products." Then—sure enough—he said, "We have overcome all obstacles thanks to the thoughts of Chairman Mao. By the authority of the Chinese Communist Party we are going to launch a campaign for young pioneers and we intend to go even further. We are determined to support the struggle for freedom of the Vietnamese people and of all the peoples of the world thanks to the quality of our excellent products."

Those who had been listening looked absolutely hypnotized with boredom; Shin's mumbled translation failed to reach heart, mind, or eardrum.

But even M. Chapeau had been most impressed by the visit, if not by the speech. At my invitation he questioned the manager. The result might have been a dialogue between two deaf men, so little relation was there between the questions and the answers.

112

CHAPEAU. How many printing machines have you got?

THE MANAGER. What matters is not the number of machines, but the total output.

CHAPEAU (*imperturbably*). Do you use the automatic frame technique?

THE MANAGER. We have no automatic frames, but we have assembly-line production.

CHAPEAU. Are your frames operated by hand?

THE MANAGER. Our materials are printed in an assembly line.

CHAPEAU. Are your machines equipped with copper rollers?

THE MANAGER. That is difficult to explain. We shall see.

CHAPEAU. Are the dyes you use imported or produced in China?

THE MANAGER. The raw material is produced in China.

I got the impression that our worthy guide was no more the manager of his mill than I was an acrobat, and that his job was more concerned with spreading the thoughts of Chairman Mao than with printing fabrics.

Having crossed a large open sports ground, we entered an apartment house. A narrow cement staircase led to a room twelve feet long containing a washbasin and four beds, each with a floral eiderdown folded in four at the foot. Four girls greeted us with smiles and little gestures of welcome and asked us to sit down on one of the beds. The room was decorated with two calligraphed posters, which looked to me like abstract paintings. Although the white paint was flaking off the walls, the room was clean and austere. Obviously it seemed very comfortable to these girls, who had probably never known electricity or running water before. Naturally most of my companions sneered at what they saw, and I wondered how many of them had ever set foot in a working-class house in their own country. In spite of good intentions on both sides the conversation was only a smiling pantomime. Our four round-faced hostesses escorted me to the door of the apartment building, where they and their friends examined me with benevolent curiosity, touching each article of my clothing in turn. As usual my shoes and stockings interested them most.

● ● ●

A loud burst of applause came from inside the big circus tent. As I was bringing up the rear of the party and was still outside in the rain, I assumed that the show had already started. I was wrong: the applause was for Boilèle, who was proudly leading the way, chin up like a real *duce,* and it stopped only when the last of us had sat down. It was ironic and amusing to see all those faces smiling, all those calloused hands applauding a solid phalanx of well-to-do bourgeois laced with textbook examples of reactionary capitalism. You almost wanted to tell those people that there had been a misunderstanding, that we were not "relatives of Uncle Mao," and that there were no more than two or three among us who liked them or even wanted to understand them. The audience seemed to be largely composed of workers and peasants. Their dark-gray or blue clothes were sometimes patched or darned, but always clean; their faces were drawn with fatigue, their eyes were weary, and their bodies were often bent by hard work and insufficient food. There were some young men and women but the majority were middle-aged and had deeply wrinkled faces; there were many sleeping children being rocked in the arms of grandmothers with bound feet and black tunics. Everybody was silently nibbling apples, nuts, little cakes, peanuts, or sesame seeds. Many kept turning around in their wooden chairs to smile, and leaning to one side to get a better view of us.

The show began with a roll of drums and a clash of cymbals. The acts followed each other swiftly—animal trainers, cyclists, and acrobats as quick and graceful as sprites. We were charmed by the lighthearted humor and witty fantasy, which are unusual in China. Even the clowns, whom I always find boring or sinister, were funny. The men's costumes were covered with sequins, and the lively, feminine girls were dressed in light-colored silk pajamas.

We applauded frantically. The delighted audience looked at us, smiled with pleasure at our enthusiasm, and clapped louder than ever.

At a drum roll the sprites skipped out, and into the ring came a pale-faced creature with a long nose and red-rimmed eyes, wearing a GI uniform and brandishing a fistful of dollars. A Chinese worker dressed in blue struck the GI with the back of his hand and sent the bank notes flying. Then, in the course of a painful pantomime, he beat the American until he bit the sawdust. The spectators in front of us turned around and looked at us, not aggressively but inquisitively and unsmilingly. They applauded. We didn't move a muscle. Yuan, Shin, and Shu didn't applaud either. A trio of women acrobats dressed in gaily rustling pajamas then bounced into the ring; they all wore lipstick and had long shining hair. They displayed the most amazing dexterity and courage.

Apart from the vulgar and distressing number about the GI, this little provincial circus was a thousand times more elegant, original, and skillful than any performance under a Western big top.

115

It was pouring rain in the morning. Muffled against it in raincoats, boots, and umbrellas, we looked like a battalion of skin divers. I had a spinach-green umbrella, bought in Loyang, that sprang open like a switchblade at the slightest pressure from my finger. In my luggageless condition it was a comforting toy. The fertile loess, turned brown by the rain, was completely deserted for miles around. In the muddy village streets a few peasants in black rubber capes wore boots; the rest were paddling about in their habitual felt slippers.

We had traveled four thousand years into the past. In 1953 a laborer had discovered the Neolithic village of Pan-Po. Thinking that he had unearthed the remains of a tomb, he had obeyed the instructions given to all workers in such a case and had informed the foreman in charge of the building site, who had in turn alerted the archaeological service. The result was the excavation of two thousand square yards of a five-acre town, exposing the outlines of streets and the circular or square foundations of houses.

The archaeologists had surrounded their excavations with an observation balcony and covered them with a huge glass roof. Most of my tourists didn't seem to find the excavations either thrilling or thought-provoking. The chill and the damp had made them grumpy. As usual it was the Blums, Georges Wolf, Chapeau, Claire Adjouf, and a sneezing Laure who remained thoughtfully on the balcony. Pariet told us that the T'angs had begun excavations in China as far back as the tenth century. In 1920 French archaeologists resumed the work that had been abandoned for a thousand years and pirated some of their finds. Abandoned once more in 1937 during the Japanese invasion, excavations were renewed only in 1950 on the initiative of the new regime. Today, he said, China is studded with excavation sites.

From my observation point I noticed the beautiful Isabella fluttering her eyelashes and talking softly to Shin. Poor chaste Shin was blushing more and more deeply, but at the same time was clearly delighted.

In spite of the rain, Shin insisted on taking us to see the hot springs that rise out of a nearby mountain, where the rival of poor Wu Tai (the unfortunate empress who had had her hands and feet cut off) had been fond of taking the waters with her imperial lover. There a series of pagodas clung to a hillside, and willows wept into an artificial lake carpeted with dead leaves. Rose petals kept drifting down to the sodden ground, and the sky was leaden. Chilled to the marrow, we crossed an arched

117

bridge and entered the favorite's pagoda, which was furnished with the sort of bed and dressing table you would expect to find at an elegant spa.

Then we jumped a thousand years to the pagoda from which Chiang Kai-shek had been kidnapped by one of his former officers who had sided with Mao. In the middle of the night of December 12, 1936, Chiang, dressed only in pajamas, had attempted to escape the trap in such haste that he had left behind his false teeth and his glasses on his bedside table. We were shown his hard, narrow bed, and we slipped and slithered in the mud to the spot where Chiang had been captured at the foot of a tree. It was all rather sinister.

After a long confabulation I finally persuaded Yuan to swap a visit to the local military academy for another visit to the museum—to the general joy of my pilgrims, who clearly found the past more attractive than the present.

In the afternoon we took shelter under the corrugated iron roof of a little market, where a host of little stalls displayed gimcrack treasures: scissors shaped like butterflies' wings, oval wooden combs decorated with pen-and-ink drawings of pagodas or junks, and umbrellas and parasols made of varnished straw, strips of wood, and oiled parchment. At the far end of the market there was an unusual shop-window containing two black wigs, a pith helmet, and a British naval officer's cap. It was a theatrical costume shop, with stacks of "imperialist uniforms," Chinese costumes of the *ancien régime* for landowners and mandarins, long silk dresses, more wigs, false beards and moustaches, rubber machine-guns and wooden pistols. My delighted tourists moved in. Boilèle in a false beard looked more like a "wicked imperialist" than ever. Isabella, Signora Coli, and I bought blue silk pajamas with wide legs, like those the acrobats had worn at the circus. The stallkeeper was at once petrified and overjoyed; he obviously thought we were "friends of Chairman Mao," but rather crazy friends judging by the frenzy with which we were buying up his stock. He finally decided that we must be a troupe of actors, as Shu told me later, much amused.

I quietly slipped away to stroll the streets of Sian. To my surprise the shopkeepers called out and beckoned me in the friendliest way to look at their wares, whereas they always showed a hieratic reserve when we were in a group accompanied by our interpreters. As soon as I left the main avenue I floundered along muddy, narrow streets lined with huts. Through the open doors I caught glimpses of cramped, squalid rooms with about a dozen people in each, chiefly old people looking after children.

When I got back to the bus, Shin was frowning. "Where have you been?" he asked. "I was worried about you."

"Oh, come now, Shin," I said with a smile. "I'm in no danger here."

I told him about my excursion into the China of dirt and poverty, the China that had so far been hidden from us. With some annoyance he explained that twenty years ago all the streets in China had been as sordid as the ones I had just walked through and that it had been impossible to get rid of them all in seventeen years. The government, he added solemnly, was faced with a gigantic housing problem and it was natural that the first to benefit should be the young, both married and unmarried, since they were the life and strength of the country, and their productive efficiency was paramount.

Later, from the top of a tower dominating a green-tiled Ming pagoda, I looked down on the maze of alleys I had walked through. The peasants' big round straw hats looked like water lilies floating on a gray lake. It was

119

the exotic China of my childhood dreams: an eternal, gray harmony that today's regime, with its ruthless efficiency, would, I felt sure, never efface.

The director of the Sian tourist service, Mme. Li, gave us a sixteen-course dinner accompanied by speeches and toasts. She was about forty, with a strong face and a dazzling smile—really a beautiful woman in spite of her hair, which looked as if it had been cut with a pruning knife, and her gray gabardine suit. I felt a little sad at being unable to inquire about her origins, her past, her opinions.

We boarded the train again for another twenty-six-hour journey—this time to Nanking. The familiar loess hills slipped by in the rain, looking like huge sand castles attacked by the rising tide. The Siberian virus had gained ground, and there was a general feeling of torpor. The previous day Adrienne had told me that she felt very ill and that she simply had to have a compartment to herself. Accustomed to her bouts of hypochondria, I had refused pointblank. According to Torti, my companions had then laid bets on which of us would win. I told the Chinese that Adrienne's demands struck me as contrary not only to their socialist community spirit, but also to the rules of good behavior in the West.

A few moments after the train left the station, Adrienne began whispering to Shin. Ten minutes later she looked me up and down with triumphant disdain from a compartment of her own.

Beside myself with rage, I collared Shu. "Where are you sleeping tonight, Shu? Here?"

"No, madame," she replied. "I've got a seat in the next compartment."

"My dear Shu," I said, "I must apologize for the chore I'm going to inflict on you, but I'd be grateful if you would share the compartment of Madame Mandois, who isn't feeling very well. Besides, it strikes me as rather embarrassing for her, with regard to her companions, to have a compartment all to herself."

My roommates, Laure, Colette, and Señora Neralinda, were delighted to have won their bet, even if I had cheated a little.

The loess hills were succeeded by fields of corn and maize and then by rice paddies—not a single road, not a single car, not a single truck. There were a few mud tracks and carts drawn by men: draft animals were obviously less common here than in the north. The farther southeast we traveled the warmer and stickier it got. We barricaded the door of our compartment to avoid being awakened by the teapot comrade. Chinese trains travel so slowly that it is easy to sleep and read on them. You can also talk, which isn't necessarily an advantage. Unfortunately, I could hear the conversations in the adjoining compartments through the partitions. Pariet was deep in a political argument with the Chinese, and his idealistic socialism struck me as incompatible with the thoughts of Chairman Mao. Pariet got excited and started shouting. I heard Shin's hesitant voice, but could not make out the words. When Pariet shouted again, I banged hard on the wall.

122

Later, in the restaurant car, Adrienne embarked on another inquisition. "Shin, what is your ambition in life?"

Predictably, Shin had no ambition.

"Come now, Shin, what would you like to do?"

Shin wanted nothing better than to serve the people.

"Shin, drop the propaganda!"

Shin, already an accomplished diplomat, declared that he was only telling the truth. His distinction and his charming manners would be sure to correct the Western picture of the Chinese Communist with a knife between his teeth and an H-bomb in his pocket.

Adrienne then turned to Noiret, who was overwhelmed by the honor and puffed out his little chest, and began again: a Dior dress cost five thousand francs nowadays. It was really impossible. Like a Chanel suit, didn't he know. A passing reference to the Rothschilds. Then Noiret dazzled even himself with what must have been an exhaustive account of all the chateaus he knew and the cost of keeping them up. Shin listened open-mouthed to this music-hall sketch, which far outdid all the anticapitalist propaganda he could ever have heard before. My toes curled in exasperation and shame.

After absorbing a large number of multicolored pills, we wished one another a good night's sleep, and I slipped delightedly into my silky acrobat's pajamas (I had already returned Georges Wolf's blue Sulka pajamas, completely faded by the Sian laundry). A restless, hot night. In the morning we were given a bowl of watery coffee and a soggy, sticky roll, which more or less summed up how I felt. At half past nine a crimson-faced Signora Leandri shouted, "Come and look! The Yangtze Kiang!"

Everybody rushed to the window and stared in disillusioned silence. Was this yellowish, muddy sea the Yangtze River, that mysterious, exotic name that had always stirred my imagination and that with other magical names

123

like "Popocatepetl," "Corfu," and "Valparaiso" had earned me high marks in geography? It was indeed, and another little dream was shattered beyond redemption.

Loud-speakers filled the huge, echoing station at Nanking with the thoughts of Chairman Mao and anti-imperialist slogans. There we were joined by the charming Mme. Fayet, the French diplomat's wife who had given us such a friendly reception in Peking. She had failed to obtain permission to accompany us to Loyang and Sian; and now when she tried to get into our bus, the local interpreter, a pimply sourpuss, rudely waved her away.

As she walked toward one of the countless cycle-rickshaws crowded around the station, I informed the local guide through Shin that unless Mme. Fayet traveled with us we would all get out. Then I pulled the poor woman forcibly into the bus.

Once the capital of China and the former headquarters of Chiang Kai-shek, Nanking is now a large industrial city and the capital of Kiangsu province. The old part of the town seemed very like Sian, with the same crowded, narrow streets, tiny houses, and colorful stalls. But the center was very different, with large squares, five-storied apartment buildings, and wide avenues. There were a great many blue and white buses, so packed with people that the overflow clung on outside. The cycle-rickshaws were all full, and at the traffic lights serried ranks of bicycles were waiting like competitors in the Tour de France.

As a special treat we were to stay at the foot of Crimson Mountain, eight miles out of town. The nearer we got to the mountain the cooler the air became, and soon the spicy perfumes of eucalyptus and orange blossoms reached us from a harmonious park studded with silvery ponds. A concert of crickets reminded me of Provence, and I was swept by a wave of foolish nostalgia.

124

Admittedly I was in poor shape: in the course of our twenty-six hours of togetherness I had attracted Laure's and Colette's germs.

The Crimson Mountain Hotel was a huge three-storied building in the style of the thirties that had been erected for Russian technicians and their families. Since their sudden departure in 1960, it had been used to accommodate tourists. It offered large rooms, a pretty garden, a vast dining room, and excellent service.

The local tourist director was about forty years old and spoke perfect American English. He was likable, gay, and frank. I was dying to ask him where he had gone to college in the States, but because we were not alone I didn't dare. He immediately agreed to my suggestion that we cancel a proposed visit to a chemical fertilizer factory, and I did not have to bury my request in the usual complimentary phrases, for he understood at once and was hugely amused. It was an enormous relief to be on the same intellectual wavelength. We were both so pleased that we laughed at each other's jokes almost behind the group's backs, like a couple of conspiratorial schoolchildren.

Boilèle and Signora Negri complained about the food —"only fit for savages" according to one; "utterly poisonous" according to the other. Laure, Colette, and the other ailing members of the party, however, were visibly perking up in the mild, dry air of the Crimson Mountain. Adrienne moaned that she hadn't slept a wink "because of that little Chinese girl in my compartment." Shu, smiling, told me what had really happened: Mme. Mandois had snored all night long like an old bear. Still, in the face of this continual whining I was finding it more and more difficult to keep my temper.

The Chinese, on the contrary, were hardly any trouble at all. I had become accustomed to the slow rhythm

125

of discussion, the importance of never openly expressing the slightest disagreement, and the absolute necessity of maintaining a fixed smile and an even tone of voice whatever the circumstances. Their propaganda and their stereotyped opinions irritated me, of course, but that was all part of the game. China, after all, is not the only country in the world whose propaganda makes visitors wince.

In the scented afternoon air we walked up the long "Alley of the Mings," where warriors and animals twice as large as life peered at us from the undergrowth. The park was alive with crickets and the scents of Provence. We finally reached the huge white stone tomb of Sun Yat-sen. It had been built by a Frenchman, but our Chinese escort made no mention of the fact—whether on purpose or simply out of ignorance it was impossible to tell. The mausoleum reminded me of the horrible Victor Emmanuel Monument in Rome.

Shin and Isabella climbed the steps to the tomb side by side. Shin was blushing and smiling shyly. Isabella looked delightful, with her peaches-and-cream complexion and her long hair. I mischievously drew attention to her slightly slanted eyes and asked Shin, "Don't you think Isabella looks Chinese, Shin?"

"Not a bit," he replied in a panic. But he gave her another long stare, just to be sure.

The afternoon drifted by, lazy and golden. I finally reached the temple of Lin-Kau, a massive gray stone building with a two-tiered roof of dark gray round tiles. The doors had modified trefoil arches; the roof was supported by stone consoles, and the crest of the roof was lined with dome-shaped Buddhist stupas. The general effect was massive, sober, and beautiful. This was the only monument I saw in China that showed signs of a marked foreign influence—chiefly North Indian.

Darkness fell swiftly, and there was a chill to the air.

Colette was coughing, Boilèle was grumbling, Adrienne was moaning, and Laure stayed behind in the bus. I felt as if I were fighting a guerrilla war, with the Chinese germs outmaneuvering my expensive American vitamins.

In the foyer of the hotel Boilèle complained shrilly, "It's a scandal! I've never heard such nonsense. What do you mean, I can't have a taxi? Madame Modiano, will you please insist on them getting me a taxi!"

Shu looked sullen, so I played the part of the ham in the sandwich once again. "Where do you want to go?" I asked.

"I want to do the antique shops," shouted Boilèle.

"Dear Mademoiselle Shu," I said, "I think that General de Boilèle wants to visit your splendid antique shops. Do you think you might do me the favor of finding a car for him?"

Shu immediately smiled, and pulling her hands out of her pockets, replied, "Of course, Madame Modiano. You shall have one immediately."

A confabulation with the comrade porter followed. As Shu was several rungs above him in the hierarchy of workers, the comrade porter fetched a pale-green Peugeot 404 to collect Mme. Trollan and General de Boilèle.

This incident confirmed my suspicions that my Chinese colleagues had decided to protect me from the wrath of my pilgrims. Nine times out of ten, in the course of the conference that followed our arrival in a new town, I had my way—which led me to think that my trio considered me a hard-working proletarian like themselves, but one unfortunately at the mercy of unrepentant capitalists. A little remark of Shin's after one of Boilèle's explosions had put me on the right track. "It is interesting for me," he had murmured, "to see how capitalism still exploits the working class in the West, poor Madame Modiano."

127

I had been appalled, touched, and rather irritated by what he said. He felt sorry for the proletarian being exploited by a capitalist, but not for Colette Modiano being shouted at by a boor. He was indignant at what he took to be a class conflict; in fact it was simply a display of bad temper on the part of one ill-bred man.

On the other hand I realized that I could turn this situation to my advantage throughout the rest of the tour. Their sympathy plus my one suit, which eventually began to look like a uniform, helped to integrate me with the "monoclad" community to which all four of us belonged.

My bedroom had a large window overlooking a walled garden planted with pale-green trees and bright-colored flowers. At half past seven in the morning the sunshine and scented breeze flooded the room. But my throat felt as if it were on fire and my legs were like rubber. I had the white face of a clown and the red eyes of an albino rabbit. Temperature: 101°. That day we were to visit an agricultural commune and a fan factory. I badly wanted to visit a commune, but the idea of see-ing and hearing my flock all day long was simply unbear-able. Because only four or five of them would really be interested in the problems and achievements of an agri-cultural commune and because Pariet was an expert on the subject, I banged on the wall to call him. I put on my best hacking cough, and only a hoarse whisper of a voice emerged from my poor body. Pariet, completely taken in, expressed alarm and anxiety. I entrusted the party to his care with a whole series of futile recom-mendations: "Don't let Boilèle monopolize you. Don't let them hang around too much—it makes them tired. Keep an eye on Laure. Explain the principle of the commune to the Blums and the Adjoufs. Don't neglect the Cha-peaus just because they're shy. There's no problem with

128

the Musketeers. Prod the others a bit and cut short the stupid questions. Try to get a discussion going with the Chinese."

The dining room was next to my room, and the shouts of the waiters and the noise of crockery traveled along the corridor in a cascade of echoes. I tottered as far as the door and said *"Nikao"* ("Good day") to the first waiter who went by. He stared at me in blank surprise when I asked him in English for my breakfast. In picture language I drew a coffeepot with steam escaping from the lid and I added drawings of apples, rolls, and a pot of jam. The man went off, looking as pleased as Punch, and came back three minutes later, shaking with laughter and carrying a superb breakfast tray. I mimed my sad condition—again to his intense amusement—and from then on he looked in every hour with tea, then apples, then more tea, then lunch, then a flower. About six o'clock in the afternoon he introduced me to his comrade successor, who said *"Nikao"* and brought me a banana, tea, dinner, and finally his best wishes for a good night's sleep. And whenever he entered, the comrade successor too started chuckling. I found the same kindness and the same genuine sense of humor almost every time I had a repeated contact with the Chinese.

Despite the fever, I had a luxurious day of reading, sleeping, and doing my nails and hair. As large blue shadows lengthened in the garden Mme. Fayet came to feel my pulse, and the rest of my flock invaded the bedroom. Georges Wolf presented me with an old painting on silk he had just bought, and Alexandre Dupont gave me a hand-painted fan. They all looked pleased to see me and said they had missed me. Even Adrienne posed theatrically in the doorway. After my lovely stolen day, I was happy to see them once again.

The next morning we boarded a train for Shanghai. For the first time Chinese passengers shared our compartment, and from their gabardine clothes I concluded that we were in a de luxe car. The seats were arranged in pairs and faced each other across a central corridor. Between each pair a vase of chrysanthemums stood on a table covered with an immaculate embroidered cloth. We were soon laughing helplessly to see ourselves jolting about like the travelers in the Hollywood version of a stagecoach. Our seats, designed for little Chinese bottoms, were extremely narrow, and we were forced to sit bolt upright. Mme. Chapeau nodded off. General de

Boilèle, bouncing up and down like an old tennis ball, kept bumping his chin on his chest. In her hieratic silence Adrienne for once was almost impressive. Georges Wolf kept sneezing. In spite of the heat he was wrapped in a medley of cashmere shawls, skillfully graded from beige to moss green. The others were reading, talking, or playing cards, except for Isabella, who kept staring obliquely at Shin.

Shin was explaining that China had nine political parties, which all enjoyed proportional representation in the National Consultative Assembly. Our skepticism was measured by our profound silence. Shin went on imperturbably, "The widow of President Sun Yat-sen is vice president of the Consultative Assembly."

"I seem to remember," I broke in, "that she is the sister of Madame Chiang Kai-shek and that both women are the daughters of a rich banker named Soong."

"That is correct," Shin replied rather briskly, "but Sun Yat-sen's widow immediately joined the ranks of the people and has never ceased to live in accordance with the thoughts of our beloved Chairman Mao."

Dupont asked quietly, "What would happen if Chiang Kai-shek came back to China? Would he be executed?"

At this Shin got up abruptly to consult Yuan, who was asleep with his mouth open a few seats away. When he came back he said, "If Chiang Kai-shek returned he would be well received and due honor would be paid him. If Chairman Mao considered his autocriticism to be honest, there would be nothing to prevent him from receiving an official appointment suited to his abilities, such as membership in the Consultative Assembly."

Noiret's face turned red, and he asked aggressively, "Is the Kuomintang represented in the Consultative Assembly?"

"Of course," replied Shin.

"How many members does the Kuomintang have in China today?"

Shin was embarrassed but honest. "I don't know."

"Why do you know the number of members in the Communist Party," asked Noiret, "and not in the other parties?"

"Because," came the answer, "on the anniversary of the foundation of the Communist Party, Chairman Mao announced that the Party had seventeen million members."

"Shin," Noiret continued, "do you know the date of the foundation of the Kuomintang?"

Noiret's unpleasantness struck me as unfair to Shin, who did everything he could for us in the friendliest way. I managed to divert the conversation to the scenery, which had become tropical after we had left Nanking. Fields of maize stretched to the horizon, and buffaloes drawing wooden plows waded through the silky green paddies. Both men and women wore huge round flat straw hats, which served as portable parasols. It was becoming very hot in the carriage, and the shrill music coming over the loud-speaker was giving me a headache. When I asked Shin to switch it off he went down the car asking permission from the Chinese passengers. As each one agreed I thanked him with a smile or a nod of the head. The music stopped, and so did the piping feminine voice that had been singing the praises of—guess who.

18

At last we pulled into a station that looked almost as old-fashioned and dirty as the Gare Saint-Lazare. At last we saw people running and pushing without looking where they were going. For some reason, in Shanghai I no longer felt that I was at the far end of the world. There were no flowers, no red carpet, just a bust of Chairman Mao. Could the south of China be as easygoing as the south of France?

In the reception hall a little speech of welcome was followed by a little speech of thanks. Rooms were allocated by the Chinese, and then promptly reallocated by me while we were driving through the old French quarter. The streets were crowded with one-storied or two-storied houses; there were a great many bicycles, and the shops displayed their wares on the street. Children squatted in the gutter, calmly opening their breeches, which had a large slit in them for that purpose. The classic blue overalls of the Chinese workers had been mended so often that they looked like American patch-work quilts. The men's clothes were all surprisingly dirty, their faces were more haggard, and their eyes sadder. On the other hand the women, who in the north looked like convicts and walked like wrestlers, wore close-fitting trousers and their white or floral blouses were clean. They looked almost chic as they smiled and sized up the men. Shu, her hands deep in the pockets of her baggy pants, scowled angrily and almost ignored the remarks and smiles of passers-by. She admitted that this was her first visit to the south and that she regarded people there as neither very serious nor very respectable. Her comment had a familiar ring. Moreover, it was reassuring to find that a tiny particle of human frivolity had managed to stand up to the steamroller of the revolution.

Shanghai was less like China than like a Chicago that hadn't had a single lick of paint since 1925. The Bund—the Wall Street and Fifth Avenue of the foreign colonies, the former avenue of the banks, of the leading import-export firms, and of the big hotels—was lined on one side with the dilapidated ghosts of early-twentieth-century capitalism. On the other side I saw the torn, copper-colored sail of an ageless junk.

We were staying at the famous Peace Hotel. In the past, when it was called the Sassoon Hotel, it had been restricted to whites and had been the epitome of luxury for the foreign colony. After crossing the worn carpets of the vast 1900 foyer, I tried both French and English on the porter, who spoke neither. My room, with its Gallé chandelier and threadbare velvet armchair, had the look of a shabby Ritz. The enamel of the bathtub was streaked with yellow. It was tarnished luxury, but luxury all the same. In the dining room the table linen was spotless and the silver was English; the waiters were dressed in livery. Most of them were old, very distinguished, and spoke English: the generation of transition.

After lunch an army of weasel-faced and vaguely hostile interpreters took us up to the roof terrace of a tall hotel that had been first a brothel for American troops from 1945 to 1949, then a hostel for the families of Russian technicians. It stands at the junction of the Whangpoo and the Soochow rivers, and the view is superb. In the distance the black mushrooms rising from the factory chimneys were melting into the gray mist. Motorboats and junks with yellow sails plied the muddy waters of the Whangpoo, which winds like a long snake alongside the gray office blocks. Just below us the British consul's residence, surrounded by a lawn and flower beds, flew the Union Jack. Set among trees and magnolias, many former European residences had been turned into schools and offices. It was easy to imagine the opulence that had once reigned side by side with destitution. The opulence had disappeared, and the destitution had become only poverty, but the impression was melancholy.

On the right, the two-storied houses built by the Europeans, the brick warehouses, and the factories reminded me of the dirty, shabby London dockland districts by the Thames.

This hybrid city, not really Chinese but no longer Western, made me uneasy. The West had brought nothing to Shanghai but poverty and suffering, and in the end had left nothing behind but a few ugly buildings that were aging badly.

As we drove once more through the former French district, our weasel-faced, twitching interpreter suddenly

135

grew venomous about the atrocities committed by the French during the colonial era. What he said was probably true, but scarcely tactful. Later I protested to his superior and obtained an apology, and the interpreter perhaps received a reprimand. For the moment he was taking the "loathsome French" to an antique shop so large that there was one department for enamel, another for ivory, a third for porcelain. The dazzled capitalists poured their yuans unstintingly into the coffers of the People's China.

The antique dealer was a charming old man who spoke perfect French and English.

"Do you own this shop of yours?"

"I have a share in it."

"How big a share?"

He lowered his eyes and pretended that he had to speak to one of his employees. Before the revolution he might also have lowered his eyes without replying, for the Chinese hate personal questions. I sympathized but I really wanted to know. I asked him if he met many tourists.

"Oh, yes!" he replied. "More and more every year, I'm pleased to say."

My tourists, like a cloud of locusts, were methodically buying up everything, department by department. Nearly all the objects were modern, but the imitations were excellent. Here and there, lost in the mass, there was an antique jewel or a few mandarin buttons in jade. I tried to imagine the fate of their original owners—a melancholy exercise. The antique dealer stopped trying to avoid my questions. He even seemed pleased to rediscover the scent of a past that must have been much more pleasant for him than the present.

"The fact is," I said mischievously, "you're a capitalist of the new regime!"

136

"To a certain extent that is true," he said with a smile. "In any case I have an enviable situation. I am very fortunate."

The reply was rather vague, but I had discovered that what the Chinese don't say is often more important than what they do say. At least the antique dealer hadn't talked to me about the thoughts of Chairman Mao, or about the achievements of the revolution.

I continued my interrogation. "How was your life before the liberation compared with the life you lead now?"

He only smiled woodenly: I had gone too far. The next moment the dealer disappeared behind another counter.

Marquis Torti bought a pretty antique jewel for his beautiful companion Signora Coli. Colette added to the collection of snuffboxes she had begun in Peking. But the champion of the shopping expedition was little Señora Neralinda. While her Peruvian banker husband sat huddled patiently on a chair, vague-eyed and flabby-lipped, she rolled like a little ball between the counters, picking up, putting down, clicking her fingers, nodding her head, waving gaily to her husband. Her rapidly accumulating pyramid was a rather horrifying sight, in spite of Señora Neralinda's smiling charm and real pleasantness. It was as though she were afraid that something might escape her, as though she were buying to satisfy a gnawing inner hunger. Shu was sulking in a corner of the shop.

"I think it's revolting," she said, "the amount of money these capitalists spend for useless trinkets of the past."

"Come now, Shu," I said. "Calm down. These trinkets may be useless to them, but not to you Chinese."

"What do you mean?" she asked aggressively.

"I mean, Shu, that your economists have very cleverly enabled your foreign 'friends' to acquire your knick-knacks of the past. That provides them with a nice supply of foreign currency, which allows you to buy from abroad the machine tools, tractors, and raw materials you lack. Even if you regard her as ridiculous, you should bless Señora Neralinda and her like, who after all are unconsciously behaving as friends of China."

My little lecture enchanted Shin, but Shu remained hostile and clearly thought I was brainwashing her. They both lived in a completely closed world and had received only a fragmentary, dogmatic education. This was what made conversation with them so difficult. We were always talking to them about concepts and issues of whose very existence they were unaware. This used to infuriate Pariet, who never emerged from his abstract world of Western intellectual socialism. He had expected to sit like a little child at the feet of the marvelous Chinese intellectuals, and he was alternately enraged or depressed when he discovered that they knew and understood nothing—least of all the thoughts that he expounded to them with generous abandon.

During my short excursion into political economics, my charges had been obligingly proving my point by frantically buying almost everything that came to hand. But to see them at it gave me the same sort of vague headache as the pastry cook's boy who has eaten too many chocolate éclairs.

Then, all of a sudden, we were whisked off to the Exhibition of the Industrial Achievements of the People's China. This show was installed in a horrible gray palace built to glorify Sino-Soviet friendship. At the entrance two colossal figures of a Russian and a Chinese were locked in a stone handshake that had been impossible to loosen after the break of 1960. Walking through the

138

endless marble halls, I noted a dentist's chair, a machine for counting blood corpuscles, a few transistors, and a cheap imitation of a Simca 1000, which fascinated our Chinese companions.

"You haven't got a car like that in France," Shin told rather than asked me. Propaganda and obscurantism. I said that I had a car, and that so did many French people, including workers. I took care not to describe a traffic jam in the rush hour. I knew that he trusted me and I did not want to arouse a chauvinistic reaction in him or make him think I was blowing some capitalist trumpet.

Our conversation was interrupted several times by Boilèle, who kept complaining loudly, "Shanghai's a terrible bore—it's all modern. The program has been bungled: we're staying here too long. Madame, change the timetable and let's leave earlier."

Adrienne was groaning that she was tired and that her feet hurt. Georges Wolf was a little depressed and looked sad. Alexandre Dupont was propping up Laure, who was smiling all the time and insisting on seeing everything. Faced with a model of a refinery, she and I agreed that there was something pathetic and admirable about this frenzied effort to survive the Russians' departure and China's present isolation in the world.

With every passing day I grew more curious about this nation that had emerged from nothing and was keeping its head above water at the cost of enormous effort. But the farther we penetrated into the heart of the country, the more I realized that I understood nothing about China. Like some of my companions, I had taken the first and possibly the most difficult step by throwing out all my preconceived ideas, prejudices, superficial judgments, hasty deductions. Yet knowing nothing, I still felt a sort of affection for these little men and women who apparently also knew nothing, or rather, who knew only the essential fact of life: that every day you must struggle to survive.

I slipped out by myself at nightfall through the side door of the hotel, which opened on a street running at right angles to the Bund. It was a fairly wide avenue lined with big lighted shops full of bicycles, footballs, one-piece bathing suits for women, aluminum pots and pans, and radio sets in wooden cases. There was no sign of anything made of plastic. When I forked off to the left, the tall street lamps disappeared and the narrow street was full of soup kitchens. Each soup dealer was perched on a little stool and kept plunging a ladle into a big caldron wreathed in steam. One by one they filled little floral porcelain bowls, which they held out to their customers. For two cents I bought a serving of excellent soup that tasted of fish. I then plunged into the silent, moving crowd of tense, thin, sometimes haggard Chinese. They looked sad, or as if their thoughts were far away, and no one paid the slightest attention to me.

I came to a flea market for old clothes. On both sides of the street, stalls made of canvas, sheets of corrugated iron, and pieces of cardboard were held together with bits of string and wire. The racks offered a selection of blue cloth trousers, shirts, pullovers in thick, coarse wool, and gabardine jackets. A few quilted jackets traced the passage of inhabitants of some remote region—Manchuria perhaps. Everything was poor and shabby, but clean and never evil-smelling.

Night had fallen. When I retraced my steps the shops along the avenue were still lighted and still empty. I suddenly realized that I was being followed. The man stopped at the door of the hotel when I entered.

140

19

The Shanghai museum was crowded with rare Chou bronzes, Han and T'ang pottery, and Ming vases. When I asked the local guide where these treasures had come from, he replied that the former capitalists had "voluntarily" donated their collections.

I was not convinced of the "voluntary" nature of these gifts and I was sorry that nobody saw fit to tell us anything about the discoveries made by Chinese archaeologists, who had presumably made some contribution since 1950 to the formation of this remarkable collection.

The showcases were opaque with dust, and the objects were unidentified apart from a few labels that even Shin could not decipher and that Pariet scorned to examine, reminding me that this wasn't his province. Torti was ecstatic when he discovered a score of Chou vases—superb bronzes as big as cathedral bells.

"What a magnificent museum!" I said to Shin.

"You really think so, Madame Modiano?"

Looking rather embarrassed, he admitted that he knew nothing about the art of the past. It was evidently no more his province than Pariet's.

"You mean it doesn't interest you?"

"No, not in the least. It isn't important and it distracts us from our principal aim," which was, of course, "the fulfillment of the thoughts of Chairman Mao."

I noticed two or three little men in their forties, wearing caps—presumably workers—and farther on, a group of silent children and I asked Shin, "Those people over there seem to be taking an interest in the futilities of the past. Who are they? Dangerous reactionary revisionists like us?"

Shin swung around abruptly, saw that I was smiling, relaxed, and finally smiled too. "Madame Modiano, you are terrible. It's impossible to talk seriously to you. You joke all the time."

Unfortunately for me, he didn't.

After the museum and before lunch my charges wandered off to shop, and I slipped out for another solitary walk, this time along the Whangpoo. Strolling beside a river is the best way I know to size up an unknown town. It is by a river that people idle away their time and abandon themselves to their emotion of the moment. Facing the water stood a boy with his arm around the neck of a girl in pigtails. This was the first time since arriving in China that I had seen a couple displaying their affection in public. A group of tired men in clean blue trousers and white shirts walked past, staring at me with hostility. It was the first time this had happened too. A little farther on, four girl students carrying books under their arms

142

laughed openly as they passed. I was beginning to feel a little ill at ease. Then a stooped man with hollow, ashen features gave me a look of real hatred and spat noisily in my direction. I reflected that this hatred for whites was simply the result of decades of racist colonialism and economic exploitation that the Western nations had practiced in China.

As I was crossing the Bund on my way back to the hotel, a cycle-rickshaw stopped in front of me, and with a tired gesture its cadaverous driver invited me to get in. The regime had clearly not eradicated individuality in the south so completely as in the north.

In the afternoon we installed ourselves in a line of long black Soviet-made cars for a tour of a new district and an old one.

We drove down a long avenue lined with little hovels that lacked even chimneys. The tiny cast-iron brazier on the pavement in front of each house served as both cooker and heater. The cars stopped at a crossroads, where a woman with the serious, unlined face of a nun shook hands and assured me that our visit was a great honor for her district; she administered the district of Shanghai called Tien-Shau. As she led the way along the main street, which the rain had turned into a quagmire, she explained that before the liberation this area had been a mosquito-infested swamp whose wretched inhabitants had been decimated by epidemics. She pointed to a mud hovel like those we had seen earlier beside the big avenue and said that it had been typical of the district in the past. Now the huts were disappearing one by one, and the local council was rehousing the families in other, modern districts.

An old, smiling woman greeted us on the threshold of her poor dwelling. A bicycle was propped against one wall. A little radio in brown Bakelite occupied a place

143

of honor on a rough table, which was presumably also used for the cult of ancestors. There was no running water, and the floors were beaten earth. The neighboring huts were similar, some thatched, others covered with broken-down tile roofs. It was a typical shantytown scene, but without shantytown smells. Everything was clean and tidy and well swept. The inhabitants wore patched but clean overalls and black felt slippers.

We made a brief stop in a reception hall, a long whitewashed room that also served as a library, studio, and cultural center. A television set in one corner was protected by a cardboard box. The walls were covered with garish posters showing Negroes, Chinese, and Arabs shaking their fists in unison at some invisible enemy. Punctuating her monotonous tirades with jabs of her right forefinger, our guide informed us that we were on the site of the former district crematorium.

In spite of the slowness of the translation and the inevitable praises of Chairman Mao that studded our hostess' speech, almost all my pilgrims seemed fascinated by this encounter with a concrete social situation. Only Boilèle and Adrienne kept shifting in their seats and grumbling.

Our hostess said that many of the local inhabitants had come to Tien-Shau from even poorer districts. Worker Sun Yen-sion, for example, who lived in lodging No. 7 in the fourth subdivision, had formerly shared an area of twelve square yards with six members of his family. The rain had leaked into his hut. Now he occupied an area of nineteen square yards and enjoyed the use of sanitary equipment. Carpenter Chou Mei-tsung lived with his wife and four children in lodging No. 10 in the fourth subdivision. He was earning $48.00 a month and had been able to buy a radio ($16.80), a bicycle ($48.00), and even a watch ($24.00). Before the libera-

144

tion, he and his family had had barely enough to live on and nothing to spare for clothes. Now they had clothes and furniture. Their monthly rent was between $0.04 and $0.06 a square yard for the living room. Water and electricity cost them between $0.08 and $0.12 per person per month.

This simple, factual exposé was a thousand times more moving than any Maoist parable. We all knew that people had starved to death in the streets by the thousands in China, as they still do today in India. Whether we like Mao's China or not, nobody dies of hunger there anymore.

I looked closely at this woman's serene, waxen face while she told us the story of a third worker. Her dogmatic faith annoyed me, but I was getting used to that, and I reflected that her only reason for living was the hardest and noblest task in the world—to ensure first the survival and then the livelihood of a few of her compatriots. I concluded that our Western form of democracy was a luxury that only well-fed peoples could allow themselves.

The right forefinger wagged like a metronome. "Since the liberation," our hostess said, "even human nature has changed in China. People have become honest. This year, in our district alone, two thousand pieces of lost property have been returned to their owners. What is more, everybody here helps his neighbor, ignoring his own interests. True, the present standard of living is still very low, but it is much higher than it used to be. In any case, the people are aware that they are building up the country under the leadership of Chairman Mao Tse-tung and the Communist Party, in whose hands they have placed themselves entirely."

"Have you a cultural center?" asked Adrienne, suddenly waking up.

145

"This is it," replied our guide. "We put on performances organized by local amateurs: plays, songs, poetry competitions, and also television and movies."

I suspected that Adrienne had heard the expression "cultural center" somewhere and was now tossing it off with only the vaguest idea of what it meant.

"What does the sanitary equipment consist of?" asked Colette Quesnel.

"Each lodging has a toilet but not a bath. There are several families on every floor."

"What proportion of the population," asked Pierre Adjouf, "is made up of children?"

"About fifty per cent."

Walking along a muddy yellow path we came to a single-storied dining hall for the retired people of the district. The retirement age was fifty for women and sixty for men. Inside, about thirty men and women were playing cards, sitting in groups of four around wooden tables. As we came in they stood up, smiling and clapping. Some of them looked old and worn out, but several struck me as hale, hearty, and still capable of working.

I asked if the old people had any occupation. Did they look after children, for instance, as sometimes happened in the north?

"No," our guide replied proudly. "For them, retirement means a rest after a working life that has often been very hard."

As we toured the district, a claque of children and young teen-agers sprang into action. Whenever our column appeared they broke into a storm of applause. When we left, the crowd drew back to allow our cars to move away. Then a bunch of children clustered around and pressed their noses against the car windows; they were alive with curiosity and responded warmly to our good-by waves.

As we drove past a four-storied concrete apartment building—it was new and unoccupied, but its balconies were already yellow with damp—I learned that the government had been able to rehouse one million residents of Shanghai. Nine million others were still waiting.

In Paris people had told me wonderful things about the Children's Palace in Shanghai. "The children are the triumph of Red China," they had said. "They are absolutely adorable."

In fact, there are twelve Children's Palaces in Shanghai. The one we visited had formerly been a wealthy merchant's residence. With its staircase of polished wood, its dark paneling, and its multicolored floor tiles, it looked very much like a luxurious Paris town house built about 1900. Massed in the doorway, twenty children grabbed each one of us by the hand, recited a little compliment in a loud voice, and relentlessly dragged us after them. Liberation was out of the question; a sweaty little paw held my hand like a vice.

In a succession of rooms children were drawing or playing cards, chess, or jackstraws. The best drawings, all in a very academic style, had been pinned on the walls. In one room we interrupted a concert of Chinese music. Fighter aircraft were dangling from the ceiling of the scale-model room. In the military training room a boy was learning how to handle a submachine gun, and a little girl of seven was crawling under a barbed-wire entanglement fitted with little bells—without making them tinkle.

"This is to ensure our defense in the event of attack," the guide said.

I gave a sudden start. Signora Negri was shrieking in the next room. "It's disgraceful training children for war! By teaching them your aggressive attitudes you'll start something horrible, and God will surely punish you."

147

"Be quiet, Mama," whispered Isabella, shaking her mother by the arm. The poor woman was completely hysterical and went on shouting about God and religion. Pushing everybody aside, Isabella and I dragged her into the table tennis room. Table tennis is the national sport of China, and Shin, impassive but still pink with emotion, reminded us that the world champion was a Chinese. In the huge glass-walled room the sound of the balls was like machine-gun fire. Adjouf, deciding to show off his skill, was pulverized by a little girl of twelve, who slowed down at a discreet signal from Shin. Suddenly Shu sidled up to me like a little shadow and said, "You are wanted on the telephone from Paris, and so is Madame Quesnel. We must go back to the hotel immediately because the telephone connections are cut off at six o'clock, twenty minutes from now. There's a car waiting outside."

I left Pariet in charge and rushed after Shu, paying silent tribute to an organization that could instantly locate a single individual in a city of ten million inhabitants.

In less than a quarter of an hour we reached the hotel, which was on the other side of the city. I beat Colette to the phone by a short head, and there indeed was Paris—a Paris that came to me in alternate waves of sound and silence. I had to fill in the blanks, but it was wonderful to hear that voice from the other end of the world speaking in such a familiar language. I came out of my room radiant, to find Colette utterly disconsolate. There was only one line, and the connections had been cut off after my call.

148

The following day the Musketeers, the Adjoufs, and Laure were going with Pariet to see a people's commune, while the Chapeaus and the Blums wanted to visit a factory. Boilèle decided to take the Italian ladies around the antique shops. So much the better—he was really becoming a pain in the neck. Signora Leandri and Colette Quesnel wanted to go to the university with me. Adrienne hesitated, then, to my dismay, decided on the university.

After a dreamless night and a luxurious breakfast in bed, I met my teammates, who were all in excellent spirits. Even Adrienne simpered pleasantly, her painted face looking grotesque in this land of few cosmetics.

The dean was a woman of about thirty-five with a

gentle, intelligent face. She was waiting for us in front of the long pink-brick university buildings, which were surrounded by trees and lawns. Tea was served in a drawing room furnished with leather armchairs and a bust of Mao. The principal, a man in his forties with the face of an intellectual, gold-rimmed spectacles, and a blue tunic buttoned up to the eyebrows, recited his little "before and after" speech in a rather embarrassed monotone. But in the midst of the usual nonsense in praise of Chairman Mao, there were a few interesting pieces of information: "Forty-five per cent of the students now come from working-class families, whereas before the liberation all the students at the university belonged to the bourgeoisie. Forty per cent of the students come from families in the liberal professions, and only fifteen per cent come from the former bourgeoisie."

At Shanghai University each student could choose his department. That was not the case at other universities, where the department chose the student according to his marks, his abilities, and his health. This was particularly true in the sciences.

I asked the comrade principal if the political science students took much interest in international politics.

"Both professors and students," replied the principal, "take an interest in world affairs in order to raise their level of awareness. They study the works of Chairman Mao and Marxism-Leninism."

"Do they have any vacations?" asked Colette Quesnel.

"Yes, five weeks every semester, which they spend in a factory or an agricultural commune. And every five years the professors are required to devote an uninterrupted period of two months to manual labor."

"Why?" asked Colette.

Because, unfortunately, of the continuing influence

of the corrupt old bourgeois society, its contempt for manual labor, and its erroneous belief in the superiority of intellectual work. After spending some time in a paddy or a textile mill, the intellectuals lose their class arrogance and feel greater understanding for the manual workers. "That is why the foremost members of the government, and even our beloved Chairman Mao, have taken part in building our dams and laying down our railways."

The principal, looking morose and irritated, repeated this last sentence three times. Or perhaps our halting interpreter knew only a single speech in French? We were treated to superficial "before and after" comments about every laboratory, every building, every department of the university. Leaning farther and farther back on his sofa, the principal recited his litanies with obvious boredom. I dreaded the moment when he would ask us to point out his deficiencies and favor him with our criticism, as a token of friendship, of course. As the principal droned on, a toothless old man in black slippers refilled our teapots with boiling water. He was very well trained, and must have served the rector of the "contemptible university" that had existed before the revolution.

In the old days the university had indeed been "contemptible," since the rich Chinese had preferred to send their sons to Europe or America. The new regime's achievements spoke for themselves, and the pompous principal's attempt to prove too much with the same everlasting arguments could only weary the most sympathetic and open-minded listeners. He continued, "All the subjects that didn't exist before—biology, biochemistry, biophysics—are taught here today."

"Even nuclear physics?" asked Colette.

"No, not yet," growled the principal.

Were research students free to choose their field of study?

151

"They are free to choose the subject of their research in conformity with the requirements of the state," was the enigmatic reply. We were told that all the professors and their families lived at the university, paying a rent equivalent to 4 per cent of their salary; that all the students were lodged free of charge; and that 70 per cent of them —the proportion that came from poor families—were given free board as well. About one third of the students were girls, and the greatest number of them studied biology. Each student had about twenty hours of lectures every week, in the mornings, and twenty-eight hours of private study.

At ten past eleven a shrill bell announced the end of the morning lectures. Walking four abreast, the students crossed the lawn like a long blue ribbon. We followed, a motley and incongruous group in that world of blue uniformity.

"I want to see a French class and an English class," Adrienne insisted with her habitual delicacy.

The pediment of the school of modern languages was adorned with mottoes in English: "Develop yourself morally, physically, and intellectually," and "Be cultured workers with socialist minds." With Signora Leandri bringing up the rear like a fat seal trailing its flippers, we took our places on the benches of a language laboratory. Each desk was equipped with headphones that relayed a text in English, French, German, or Russian. The French voice, distinguished and rather theatrical, recited a passage from Karl Marx about the achievements of the working class that was extremely rich in vocabulary. Instead of a blackboard there was a screen; we were shown a film with a commentary in English about the increase in steel and petroleum production and the construction of a chemical fertilizer factory.

The next room was like a radio studio. Adrienne

pounced on the microphone and instantly recited a trite little speech in which she spoke of her joy at being there and of the happiness she wished all her listeners. Her rhetoric was carried by loud-speakers to the four corners of the university. Colette and I squirmed with embarrassment, but the Chinese never batted an eyelid. Their absence of any sign of emotion was sometimes very comforting.

The students' library was a large, well-lighted room furnished with wooden chairs and tables and lined with Chinese books. An official was translating a beautifully calligraphed saying of Mao's: "Flames can set fire to a plain." On a wooden bulletin board was the familiar poster showing a Negro, a Chinese, and an Arab brandishing their fists. At the top of the poster was a caption in English: "Freedom now."

Another bulletin board displayed photographs taken in Cuba and Czechoslovakia. One of them showed Filipinos waving a banner that said, "CIA public enemy No. 1." In another, Indonesians were painting "U.S., go home" on the walls, while a third showed two American officers standing by the debris of their plane after it had been shot down over Vietnam. How poignant pictures of prisoners always are!

Outside, students were still walking past in military formation, as though the same group were going around the block and reappearing, like actors at the opera.

We next visited a white dormitory containing eight bunk beds, a large table, and eight chairs, and on the wall a huge photograph of Mao and two calligraphed posters. The only other decoration was a vase containing a couple of paper roses. The students' blankets were folded in squares at the foot of the beds. In response to my stupid question "Do you work hard?" a bespectacled young man with prominent teeth replied politely if pre-

153

dictably, "Oh, yes, we work hard for the future of the revolution, which has brought us happiness."

His English was correct, his accent reasonably good. At these words his fellow students, who were massed in the corridor, smiled and clapped. He was good Red Guard material.

We said good-by to the principal, who had not for an instant abandoned his morose expression. Was he violently hostile to foreigners? Was he secretly opposed to the regime? Or was he simply suffering from an ulcer? Or all three? The frustration was that we would never know.

As we were leaving, the friendly dean who had met us on our arrival translated a few passages of a type-written paper posted on a big bulletin board. It was the autocriticism of a student who accused himself of having misunderstood Mao's order reducing by one third the political and academic activities of all students. He confessed that he had rejoiced unduly over this order because he was lazy. But now he realized that the revered chairman's brilliant edict was indispensable for the preservation of the physical and mental health of the students. There followed a long list of Mao's wise instructions.

"Ignoramuses! Utter ignoramuses!" said Adrienne, who was probably under the impression that Karl was one of the Marx brothers.

In the afternoon Yuan suggested that we visit a "repentant capitalist."

We drove through the industrial northern part of the city, along wet, narrow streets lined with leprous gray walls. Occasional gaps revealed grubby huts and muddy yards occupied by pyramids of coal. Perched on these black hills, men and women protected from the rain only by scraps of oilcloth filled tall, round baskets with coal and then loaded them onto carts.

I told our interpreter how much I admired the effort

154

being made by the Chinese people. Shin translated for Yuan, who turned around and gazed at me intensely as he answered, as if I could understand Chinese. Shin told me that Yuan was suggesting that I stay and teach French at Peking University. I guessed that this flattering proposal had not sprung spontaneously from Yuan's brain, but reflected a decision taken by the relevant authorities. I explained that I had a daughter who was still very young, but that in a few years I would be happy to return and that I would be honored to make my small contribution to the immense edifice that was China. As I said this, I noticed that not only did I express myself more and more in the Chinese way, but I nodded my head while I talked.

A water main had obviously burst, for our car threw up two sprays of black water. I ventured a joke: "Chairman Mao doesn't need to go as far as the Yangtze Kiang for a swim!"

When Shin translated what I had said, Yuan and the Shanghai interpreter seemed to be hugely amused. Yuan asked if I could swim. I replied that I could, but that he mustn't worry: Chairman Mao could soon put half the width of the Yangtze between us. They roared with laughter.

In a yard that was bigger and cleaner than the coal dumps we glimpsed on our way, a middle-aged man in a smart beige raincoat greeted us warmly, though with a hint of embarrassment. Holding me by the elbow (he was the first Chinese to touch me in any way except to shake hands), he led us through a cotton mill employing six thousand workers. Once he had owned it; now he managed it for the state. He did not offer a single technical explanation, but strode through the workshops as if he were on a grouse-moor. I was amused to see the obvious disappointment of my companions: they had

155

come to see a pathetic survivor of a defunct regime, who hated and feared the new government. Instead they were galloping along behind a portly, well-dressed gentleman who was actually ogling their guide.

At the end of the marathon through the mill the manager, without consulting the interpreter, pushed me into his private car—a gleaming black Jaguar (last year's model, my host told me). The local interpreter sat in the front seat. I began a conversation in English with our host, Wong Jong-yi, who spoke it fluently, having spent two years in Birmingham as a trainee in a mill. Without hesitation he told me that in 1949, at the outbreak of the revolution, he had fled to Hong Kong with his wife and three children. He had dreaded the arrival of the Communists, who not only stripped all the bourgeois of their possessions, but also, it was said, practiced "common ownership of women." The following year he had gone back to China to see for himself. Presumably provided with solid guarantees, he had returned to Hong Kong to fetch his wife. The children had followed the next year. He told me that he still spent a couple of weeks every year in Hong Kong, where some of his relatives were still living. He explained that since 1955 his mill had been a joint enterprise of "workers and capitalists cooperating to increase production." He spoke about the terrible poverty of the Chinese cotton workers after the war, at the time of the Kuomintang. China had then imported 90 per cent of her cotton from the United States, and the Chinese mills had served only as finishing shops for the American cloth. The smaller workshops had had to close down, and the same process, repeated in other industries, had resulted in complete economic dependence. Like a few other liberal industrialists, he felt that China could become and remain a nation only by gaining her economic freedom. That was why he had freely

156

decided to cooperate with the Communist Party, which was the only party pursuing that aim.

M. Wong seemed to be very much at ease, but it was impossible to tell whether his manner was sincere or affected. After about ten minutes the interpreter suddenly said something in Chinese, and M. Wong, with some embarrassment, immediately said to me in his excellent English, "I must apologize to you for my inadequate command of English. It would be better if I spoke in Chinese and your interpreter translated what I said."

The interpreter, of course, spoke no English. So that the manager might save face I asked him a few harmless questions in French. He promptly launched into a violent attack on Western propaganda, which was forever criticizing China. I assured him that he had no idea how much sympathy and curiosity China aroused in Western Europe, how many articles were published on the subject, and how disastrous and blameworthy the Western liberals considered the economic and political isolation in which part of the world tried to keep China. I didn't mention the United States by name, for in China more than anywhere else, you have to know how far is too far, and the United States, for the Chinese, is too far.

We carried on a commonplace and leisurely conversation until we reached his handsome house, which was full of carpets, fine lacquered furniture, chandeliers, and showcases crammed with Ch'ing porcelain. The comrade owner-manager's wife was dressed in a flannel skirt and a cashmere sweater. Two maids in black pantsuits and white aprons served tea and little cakes. Our host cut our questions short and shrilly recited a summary of our conversation in the car. He had become awkward and nervous. The lady of the house fussed over us in the

157

Chinese manner, but her humble smile was betrayed by the despotic flash in her eyes.

M. Wong assured us of the honor that our visit represented for him, especially as he received very few foreigners. I didn't believe a word of this, for I was convinced that the Chinese frequently showed their visitors this curious example of a marriage between capitalism and Communism. Our host, we learned, received an annual interest of 5 per cent on his capital as valued in 1956. This interest amounted to 80,000 yuans or $31,200 a year, which was paid to his bank. Unable to spend it all, he left three quarters in his account. He could not invest any money, buy another business, or acquire any more property, not even paintings and *objets d'art*. Twice already, in 1962 and 1965, this *modus vivendi* had been given official approval. Moreover, he could leave his house, furniture, car, and possessions to his heirs without paying inheritance taxes. He said that his was not an exceptional case: several hundred managers of big factories in Shanghai enjoyed the same advantages, and in addition, several thousand small capitalists retained partial or complete ownership of their businesses. Often the interest on the capital invested in these businesses was insignificant, and the owners had chosen to receive a fixed monthly stipend instead.

I asked M. Wong whether when he drove his Jaguar past one of his workers hitched to a heavy cart, he didn't think that in the eyes of that worker he represented the very image of man's exploitation of man.

"Of course I do," he replied. "But that worker knows as well as I do that exploitation is a contradiction of society, an abnormality, and is therefore doomed to disappear. He also knows that his life is going to improve and that exploitation cannot last because the capitalists have agreed to give their property to the people. So the

158

difference between capitalists and workers can only diminish. And that's the main thing."

My companions could hardly believe their ears. M. Wong's paradoxical way of life and opinions were completely inconsistent with their idea of what things were like in Communist countries.

With countless precautions and excuses Colette Quesnel said to our host, "Forgive me for being so indiscreet, but your case has an extra interest for us in that it might be ours one day. Has your life changed a great deal?"

M. Wong shook his head. "There is no difference between my material circumstances now and before the revolution. I have kept my house and my servants. It's my way of life that has changed. I've done with the gambling, the wasteful spending, the sophisticated life of the past. That's why my expenditure has gone down so much."

"What do your children do?" asked Laure.

"My eldest daughter," he said, "is a student in the faculty of medicine in Shanghai. She's a member of the League of Youth. My second son is studying physics at the College of Science and Technology. My two youngest children are at secondary school. None of my children wants to be a capitalist. All of them are perfectly integrated in the new society and well adjusted to their new way of life."

The material side of his life was one thing—you could believe what he said or not; in any case he was doing very well for himself. But his children were another matter. I got the impression that it hurt this apparently jovial man to see that his children were strangers whose values were different and who no longer thought as he did.

The musical-comedy maids relieved us of our teacups and served coffee.

Our host volunteered the information that old-age

pensioners received 60 per cent of their salaries after ten years' service and 70 per cent after fifteen, and that small capitalists received a high rate of interest. What was more, he explained, children were educated by the state, and material problems had disappeared. Even the small minority of capitalists who didn't work were suitably indemnified.

This middle-aged man, who had probably been a liberal to begin with and was certainly a favored citizen now, could obviously not be expected to express any sort of nostalgia. All the same, the contrast between the enthusiasm of his words and the sadness of his expression upset us all. We could sense that he was afraid of our questions, that he felt embarrassed. When I decided to cut short his ordeal he and his wife courteously accompanied us to our cars. Laure and Colette lingered for a moment to thank them effusively. Our host seemed touched, his wife delighted.

On the return trip Yuan asked me for any criticisms I might like to make. As usual I said nothing. But at the hotel my tourists began a heated argument, much of it irrelevant.

"It isn't his house," Signora Negri stated flatly.

"The car was given him by the Party only to impress visitors," declared Torti.

"Poor fellow, having to play the fool for a lot of foreigners!" sighed Mme. Chapeau.

Laure and Colette sent flowers to Mme. Wong, a kindness that didn't surprise me, coming from them, and that they were the only ones to show.

After an excellent dinner, admirably served, we boarded our bus again for an evening at the Grand Monde, formerly a giant brothel. It was an ugly gray five-storied building with balconies arranged around a courtyard. On the ground floor was a gallery of distorting

160

mirrors; on the upper floors, paved with asphalt, were crowded auditoriums where people were laughing and listening spellbound to edifying plays, clowns, and story-tellers. Stalls sold fritters, pies, sesame loaves, and noodles. A maze of other rooms were hung with draw-ings showing superstitions that ought to be abolished. It was a silent, well-behaved, happy crowd, nibbling food and indifferent to our presence. Within half an hour we had seen everything and returned to our hotel, leaving behind only the Musketeers and Pariet, all four of them probably a prey to some vague nostalgia.

On the train to Hangchow the next morning, Pariet told me that he had left the Musketeers at the Grand Monde a quarter of an hour after our departure to come back to the hotel by himself. After he had walked a few yards, a shadow had separated itself from a wall, and a man had politely offered in Chinese to take him back to the hotel, for fear that he had lost his way. Pariet, also in Chinese, had thanked him but declined the offer. In vain. The shadow had repeated that he would never 'forgive himself should a foreign friend get lost. All of a sudden Pariet had felt himself lifted off the ground and hurled onto a passing tram. The shadow had helped him off when the tram reached the hotel and had only let go of him, with a courteous farewell, outside the door, where the shadow had remained until Pariet disappeared in-side. The poor fellow was quite put out by the whole affair, and although I knew it was wrong of me, I couldn't help laughing. He was stumbling from one disappoint-ment to another, and his humanitarian liberalism was suffering from every word spoken by the Chinese. He argued bitterly with them for hours, presenting French left-wing points of view that struck them as so much gibberish. He was really quite touching, and so naive that I felt like his grandmother.

After arriving at Hangchow early in the afternoon, we drove along the shores of a lake that was sad and silvery under the gray sky. Mountains stood out in gentle silhouette in the distance. Many but unfortunately not all of our hotel rooms overlooked the lake and the gardens around it. I allotted the rooms with the view to the married couples and the women on their own, and I put the men in the rooms facing the forest. Thus Mme. Trollan overlooked the lake and her friend Boilèle had a view of the forest. A storm of Latin anger broke with a violence that jarred painfully with the halftones of the surrounding landscape. I quietly beseeched the Chinese to try to get me a few more rooms with a lake view.

162

I could feel them weakening when Noiret rushed up, as red as a turkey, and snarled, "You keep asking us for criticisms—well, I'm going to give you one now! Allow me to inform you that in France travelers are all treated the same way!"

I broke into an icy sweat. Shin, pink-faced, turned around slowly and said, "Do you mean to tell me, Monsieur Noiret, that there are no rooms at the back of French hotels?"

Boilèle then burst out of Mme. Trollan's room with a view, grabbed me by the shoulders, and started to shake me. "You always treat me worse than the others. I shall complain to your director. You wait and see what happens to you when you get back. In any case I've had more than enough of this filthy country!"

The faces of the Chinese went blank. It would have been funny if I hadn't felt so ashamed. I extricated myself from Boilèle's grip and sent everybody off to lunch, including the Chinese.

Colette Quesnel, with typical sweetness, sacrificed her lake view, which I gave to Boilèle. Then I put Noiret in the general's old room, which offered an oblique glimpse of that damned piece of water. I moved Georges Wolf, whose window looked onto a heap of coal, into Noiret's room and took the coal-hole myself.

The "Chinese table" stood up as I came into the dining room and fussed over me. Noiret was embarrassed and stared the other way. Shin looked anxious and whispered, "I think your General de Boilèle could do with a period of re-education."

Yuan spat impassively into his handkerchief. When I handed Boilèle the key to his new room he leaned back in his chair and said, "You see! I told you there'd be a way!"

The "European table" was completely silent. The

general was disavowed by his neighbors, who came over one by one to tell me so. I tried to imagine the impression all this had made on the Chinese, who considered us at best selfish and devoid of community spirit.

When we met again at three o'clock the atmosphere was still strained. Our bus drove alongside the lake, shining like a sheet of mercury in the rain and fog, to Hangchow, a town of six hundred thousand. It was a rather sad, dull place, only picturesque in a street of covered stalls selling combs, scissors, candy, soap, and ivories.

We dragged our wet feet into a brocade factory, to find only rather ugly artificial silks and some silk panels a yard wide depicting Marx, Engels, and Mao. On our return to the hotel we felt as if we were bathing in liquid mud. To soothe my nerves I went for a solitary walk in the beautiful park planted with pine trees. The turned-up roofs of the houses glistened in the rain; men and women passed in silence as night fell over Hangchow, which an ancient proverb calls an earthly paradise.

Before the revolution Hangchow had been a famous spa frequented by well-to-do Chinese. Their villas, built in the European style of 1900 on the hills around the lake, had been turned into old people's homes, sana-toriums, and nursing homes by the new regime. I thought to myself that new regime or not, a spa in the rain always gives an impression of boredom and stagnation.

By the following morning the rain had stopped. The lake and the surrounding hills were wreathed in a silvery mist and had the tranquil grayness of the tropics. Having left the town, we drove between flower beds, shrubs of different varieties, and coral trees. The road wound across wooded, terraced hills that were planted with round tea bushes studded with small white flowers. The harvest was over, but two girls mimed the movements

164

of tea-picking for our cameras. The village, or rather the commune, was very pretty, with whitewashed brick houses covered with double-tiered roofs of gray tiles. In an attractive room with dark wainscoting and a massive dark wooden table, we were given Dragon's Well tea, the most famous in China. The director of the commune, a lively little woman of about thirty, said that the commune received 60 per cent of the proceeds from the sale of its tea. She also informed us that there were thirty thousand leaves in each pound of tea, and that the best leaves were those picked during the first ten days of the first harvest. However, she did not know the price at which the commune sold its tea to the state. "That probably depends on the quality" was all she said.

The commune was extremely clean. Healthy-looking children were running about the paths. Women dressed in blue and carrying baskets smiled at us. The school shone like a new pin. The walls of the two classrooms were covered with multicolored posters exhorting the children to cut their nails, wash their clothes, 'and do exercises to prepare themselves for the "defense of the country"; others advocated "work and discipline" and declared that "Lenin is the great protector of the people."

I left the village for a solitary stroll in a bamboo forest. The slim golden stems grew several dozen feet high and were so crowded together that the sunshine came through in dazzling arrows. Two girls were washing clothes in the stream that wound along beside the path, and amazingly in prudish China, a boy was bathing naked. In the powdery light a shadow approached: it was a peasant balancing a pair of buckets on the ends of a bamboo pole he carried on one shoulder. The buckets contained pig manure, which together with 7 per cent of their land, belongs to the peasants. He was furious at being photographed and hid behind a tree.

The lake had been dredged to make boating possible, and as the afternoon gilded the water we embarked four by four in boats. Green tea was served under a canvas awning as a woman standing in the stern pushed on a long oar. The shore receded into the distance, and with it the former holiday villas, the pine plantations, and the bamboo forests. Feeling very languid, we disembarked on an island ablaze with chrysanthemums and perfumed by flowering shrubs. I crossed little arched bridges, walked by tiny pools that shone like mirrors, and finally reached the Bridge for Contemplating Goldfish, where, like everybody else, I threw bread to the fish.

Laure tore me away from the goldfish to say that Shin and Yuan had installed themselves in her boat and had surreptitiously handed her pamphlets advertising tours organized by Luxingsche, the Chinese travel agency. Yuan had said that if any of our group wished to revisit China it would be in their interest to apply to him, because their trip would cost much less than the present tour. It was a strange thing to do, and I wondered whether he wanted to sabotage a capitalist organization or whether he was fighting the profit motive, a motive considered immoral in China.

On the drive back, watching Hangchow appear all red and black in the setting sun, I thought about the human passion for comparing a new landscape to a familiar one. For Simone de Beauvoir, Hangchow was the Athens of China; for a Dominican priest named Father Lelong, it recalled Capri.

Even though it had been the capital of the Sung emperors, Hangchow did not strike me as a place where the spirit blows, not even the spirit of pleasure. It reminded me neither of Capri nor of Athens, but simply of an ordinary Chinese landscape. In any case, we had all had a pleasant and refreshing outing in the country,

166

the more refreshing because Boilèle was in bed in his room overlooking the lake with a severe attack of colic. Poor Noiret—for whom I felt some sympathy—was suffering the same agonies and looked rather green as he wandered miserably beside the lake. He was upset too because the Musketeers hadn't spoken to him since his outburst of temper the day before, and I promised to put in a good word for him. It was really rather funny to feel like a schoolmistress in charge of twenty more or less impossible brats.

That evening at the opera a Chinese Communist resistance fighter had a bone to pick with the Kuomintang and the Japanese. The audience consisted mainly of peasants; they were very poorly dressed and their faces struck me as more tired and emaciated than those in the north. One after another we all fell fast asleep. At the intermission I took half my flock back to the hotel, explaining that they were suffering from the Asian flu. During dinner, at which the service was not as good as it had been elsewhere, Laure made a tremendous scene because the tablecloth was wet. Our waiter was petrified. Was it out of spite that he brought us a revolting jelly made of lotus roots?

The next day Boilèle appeared, looking waxen. Oddly enough, I was pleased to see him, for I had been really afraid of having to trail an ailing general around with us. In spite of his weakness he managed to point a furious finger at a delegation of French-speaking Negroes embarking on the gleaming lake. "Look at that!" he roared. "Even niggers are treated better than we are. *They* get motorboats!"

The incident was a bad omen. Shin informed me that on our flight to Canton the following day we would be entitled to only fifty pounds of luggage per person. Any excess would be sent on by train—in other words it would arrive in Canton after we had left for Hong Kong. I swore loudly, embracing in a single malediction ill-bred reactionaries, stupid regulations, and even the golden lake that had caused me so much trouble.

I then announced that all excess luggage was to be left in the corridor the next morning before they went to Mass. (I had even had to find them a Mass in the heart of Red China!)

I outlined the day's program rather curtly to Pariet and left him in charge while Shu and I went to the airport to try to negotiate. When we got there we found only a new-style coolie at the check-in counter. He knew nothing and understood nothing.

While returning to the hotel I tried to soothe my nerves by concentrating on the scene before me: vegetables planted in hundred-yard squares made up an immense market garden that resembled a green and yellow patchwork quilt. The fields were being worked by groups of about a dozen peasants. When I opened the window I was struck by the strong smell of manure in the warm, humid air. Then I saw why: behind each tidy wooden peasant's hut was a big wooden bucket for human manure. Manure has always been one of the greatest riches of China, and one of its greatest sources of shame. Under the *ancien régime* hundreds of families made small fortunes by buying human manure street by street and district by district. The servants of every house would leave it in a little hut at the end of the street. Those huts have now disappeared, but human excrement is still collected in both town and country in big wooden buckets with heavy lids.

Shin told me later that the government was giving considerable attention to the construction of chemical fertilizer factories and the development of those that already existed. But for the moment, he said, the amount

168

of chemical fertilizer produced was small in relation to the needs of Chinese agriculture. Manure accordingly remains the brown gold of China.

Later, sitting on a bench by the lake writing a few letters, I attracted a score of curious children who laughed as my pen moved across the paper from left to right. They rocked on their heels, held their sides, and even wept with merriment, but without making fun of me. What I was doing just struck them as terribly funny.

Pariet had announced that in the evening he would lecture on the Sung dynasty. This talk was to be the last of a series that had often been extremely interesting. The previous lectures had been held in one of our own rooms to avoid the risk of being accused of expressing subversive opinions in public. This time, because Yuan, Shin, and Shu had asked permission to be present, we installed ourselves in one of the hotel drawing rooms, and I ordered some little cakes and a sherry-type wine to make it a small party.

Pariet opened the floodgates. Shin provided a simultaneous translation for Yuan. At the end of the lecture, while I was passing the cakes, Yuan said that he approved of the facts given by Pariet, whose standard of education he admired, but that he disapproved of the interpretation placed on those facts. There was a stunned silence.

Pariet had never had so many supporters. After a confabulation between Shin and Yuan, Shin explained his colleague's viewpoint succinctly if not very lucidly: "In the entire history of the world, it is always the people who have done everything—sharing our land, conquering countries, producing works of art—and not generals or so-called emperors."

And that was that—a curious contrast with Pariet's intelligent lecture. Noiret was getting ready to lead the snickerers into battle, so I hurriedly sounded the retreat.

On the morning of our departure, Shin and I collected the sixty suitcases as Boilèle protested loudly that nobody told him anything. I was determined to send the excess luggage by air.

We had seven hundred pounds of overweight. The plane, I was told at the airport, could not take it. I pointed out to a fairly competent young woman at the check-in desk that it was in the airline's interest to take the suitcases and make us pay an excess luggage charge, whereas if the luggage went by train no government department would receive that money. The girl reflected on this lesson in economics and plunged into her catalogues. While waiting, I wandered around the lobby, where, to my surprise, there were many pamphlets in Chinese and English about the thoughts of Chairman Mao and the war in Vietnam written by the Australian journalist Wilfred Burchett. Finally the girl emerged from her calculations and spoke to Shin, who translated, "It's agreed, but it will be very expensive. That's why they never do it."

Prepared for the worst, I asked, "How much?"

"Not quite half a yuan for every pound of excess luggage."

Eighteen cents, or a total of $126. A mere trifle! Out of politeness I looked solemn before agreeing to the price. The little peasant porters stared at me as if I were a Martian. I slowly extracted wads and wads of yuans from my handbag. The poor cashier, who had never seen so much money in her life, started counting the notes with a clumsy thumb as a crowd gathered to watch.

We boarded a Viscount with blue plastic fittings. It was gay, pleasant, and very European. There were a few Chinese passengers in gabardine suits on board, but they

170

did not seem to notice the horde of noisy Europeans who rapidly took over the plane.

The takeoff seemed so slow that I looked up from my book and saw to my alarm that only two of the four propellers were turning. I don't know very much about aeronautics, but this kind of takeoff struck me as pretty daring. Blum had noticed too, and I whispered to him to keep quiet. But Noiret had seen and started telling the others. Luckily by then we were in the air.

"It's to economize on fuel," Shin explained casually.

It occurred to me that the revenue from our mountain of excess baggage might have been the occasion for a modest splurge on fuel.

22

Two hours later the scorching humidity of Canton hit us in the face like a towel soaked in hot water. We waited in the torrid airport while the local interpreters chirped and pirouetted in a little ballet. One of them said we would spend the first night fifty miles outside Canton: every hotel in the city was full on account of a fair that had attracted two thousand foreigners. I grumbled wearily but in vain. Then a second interpreter said that for this night in the country we were to take only our hand luggage; the rest was to be checked at the airport. This time I got on my high horse.

"I'm willing to accept the difficulty in finding us accommodations because I imagine you can't do anything about that, but I refuse to agree to submit my group to considerable discomfort just because you want to avoid paying for two or three porters. That is absolutely unacceptable and I find it hard to reconcile with the traditional laws of Chinese hospitality."

Yuan kept nodding agreement throughout Shin's translation. I felt that I was strongly supported on the left, so to speak, and I pressed my point. The Cantonese had a private consultation and gave in. I began to see what a little determination could do and I successfully insisted on a drive through the city before we traveled to our distant refuge. The bus drew up outside a cool, shady park perfumed by flowers and alive with twittering birds.

"The antique shops, the antique shops," chorused Boilèle, Adrienne, and Noiret.

"What do the majority want?" I asked.

No reply. The majority wanted nothing. They had all had enough. Instead of strolling in the pretty park, we went to the local antique shop, which, as it happened, was a great disappointment. But it was situated beside the River of Pearls (so called on account of its milky color), which was crisscrossed by pretty junks whose red and brown sails, often in tatters, bellied in the warm breeze.

Canton was very lively but far from clean. In the colorful crowd, many of the men wore white shirts, while the girls wore light blouses and pants, but never skirts. Once again, the people looked more haggard than those in the north. Noiret kept digging his elbow in Dupont's ribs. "Look at the girls, old man, they're much better looking than they are in the north. That one over there is terrific!"

The strict continence of Mao's China was obviously beginning to tell on some of my pilgrims.

In the swarming poorer districts the narrow streets

173

were lined with small houses and littered with carts, cycles, stalls, and baskets. The rooms we could see into were tiny and full of women and children. There was no silence here, but squealing, shouting, arguing, swearing. The houses of the former residential districts looked like French seaside villas in 1930, except that here they were half hidden by palm trees, banana trees, and hibiscus. Nothing had been painted for twenty years; the walls were flaking, black streaks marked the façades, and washing was hanging in the windows.

Chou-Hua, the remote rural paradise where we were to spend the night, was situated at the end of a long rutted road, which we traveled at nightfall in our jolting bus. My neighbor, Georges Wolf, was shaken by violent fits of coughing. He was sweating profusely under a huge cashmere shawl and two vicuna turtlenecks. On the next seat Shin was smiling happily at Isabella. I couldn't tell whether Shu had a soft spot for Shin, if indeed it is still possible for anyone to have a soft spot in modern China, but it was obvious that she loathed Isabella. Pariet, Shu's seatmate, had fallen out with the Chinese ever since the train trip from Nanking to Hangchow, when he had lost his temper trying to win them over to his socialist-liberal-democratic-Jacobin revisionism. The poor man was very bitter and found it impossible to understand why a respect for human rights should be unknown in China. I had tried to explain to him that the Chinese system didn't work that way, but he was just as stubborn and just as sincere as my Chinese colleagues and he refused to listen to reason. On the practical level the situation was rather awkward.

The pimply, obsequious interpreter leaned toward me with a slobbering smile. "What do the French think," he asked, "of the American atrocities in Vietnam?"

Whatever I might think, I had no intention of telling

174

him. "Go to France," I said, "if you want to find out what the French think. For the moment, what interests us is China, not the United States."

The hotel garden was scented with pepper and orange blossoms, but the building itself had the damp, blotchy walls of a seedy seaside boarding house off season. In my room the curtains and the mosquito net were torn, and the water trickled cold from the faucet.

In the corridor Adrienne, wigless for once, moaned, "I want some milk and a couple of apples. That's enough for me. I'm not at all difficult. Send them up right away, won't you?"

But there wasn't the ghost of a waiter anywhere, and Adrienne later appeared in the restaurant repeating her apple litany. For the second time Shin remarked, "There are some people who would benefit from a period of re-education."

The next day we woke up in paradise. We were on the shores of a lake surrounded by paddies and forests, coral trees and orchids. After breakfast we set off again for Canton. The peasant women were arriving in a slow procession, wearing huge straw hats surrounded by a black fringe, presumably to filter the light and keep away insects. Teams of workers, stripped to the waist, were widening the road by digging up the banks of red earth that bordered it.

In the crowded, hot center of Canton, on the corner of two streets loud with shouting and the rattle of trams, we stopped in front of a doorway half closed by a corrugated shutter. This was our hotel. In a small tiled lobby with leprous walls, two boys of twenty chattered away behind a counter paying no attention at all to our arrival. The two local beatniks casually handed me cards with our room numbers and informed me that the married couples would have rooms with twin beds, but that those

175

who were traveling alone would have to sleep three to a room.

My de luxe tourists, already condemned to staying in a hovel, were now expected to sleep in threes! The two young jokers were openly making fun of me. I accused them of fraud, reminding them that our classification as luxury tourists entitled us to better accommodations. When they only snickered, Shin grew irritable. I pointed out the folly of what they were doing. "After such a successful tour, how stupid it would be to leave friends of China with an unpleasant memory. The last impression is always the most lasting. It would be heartbreaking if that impression were a bad one."

The clerks shrugged. Canton, I decided, was definitely Marseilles, with a touch of Corsica thrown in. On the other side of the counter Boilèle shouted, "This is all the fault of the Paris organization. They are responsible. If something goes wrong in my bank, I'm the one who's responsible. Well, this is the same, isn't it?"

Laure tried to calm him down. "For heaven's sake, shut up. There's no comparison. When *will* you understand that we are in China, in a completely different world?"

Colette whispered that she and Laure would be delighted to share a room with me, and that the Musketeers too were willing to room together. I was touched, but I decided to fight for the principle.

"If you don't find me ten single rooms, I promise you that I shall lodge a complaint against you in person with the embassy of the Chinese People's Republic in Paris, stating that you are sabotaging the tourist industry in southern China. I will give you a quarter of an hour."

I was foaming with rage that I had repressed for a month and I must have looked it, for the languid beatniks behind the counter sprang to their feet. One of them

176

started yelping into a telephone. It was really rather funny: I had started a positive panic. When the boy had finished phoning Shin grinned broadly and said, "You've got your ten rooms. But some German industrialists who are arriving later won't get theirs!"

It was a triumph to get my way and outdo the Germans at the same time. My squalid room was separated from an evil-smelling corridor by a cracked door with a fanlight over it. The bathroom floor was covered with a torn piece of old linoleum, and cockroaches frolicked at the bottom of a prehistoric bathtub streaked with rust. The two guards on duty on our floor were shouting at each other in the narrow hall. My window looked out on the roof of the house across the street, where two repairmen ogled me shamelessly. The polished veneer of Mao's China—clean, polite, honest, prudish, and conventional—had evidently not spread as far as Canton.

After lunch Yuan took me aside and expressed regret for the morning's incident. But he emphasized that it had not been his fault and he reminded me that nothing of the sort had happened in the north, under his jurisdiction. I told him emphatically that I was more than satisfied with his cooperation and his admirable efficiency, that I was very grateful to him for both, and that I had not failed to note the difference between north and south. Shu, standing with her hands in her pockets, broke in spitefully, "We'll never be able to do anything with these southerners. They don't even speak a language we can understand."

Subsequent events proved Shu right. The cultural revolution had its work cut out in the south, and Shanghai even became a rebel city.

We visited an ivory workshop: a series of rooms on three floors in which sixty workers were cutting, etching, and chiseling blocks of ivory with the precision of Swiss

177

watchmakers. In each room a "creator" drew the model—always a traditional design—which the other workers then carved straight from a piece of ivory. Many of the artisans looked hollow-faced and tired. A few of the women wore gold wedding rings. The men's vests often had holes in them. On the other hand, despite the heat, there were no bad smells anywhere in the workshop.

In the same street children were coming out of school in an orderly swarm, without running or shouting. Groups of "pioneers," or star pupils, wearing red neckerchiefs, stared at us inquisitively but without friendliness.

In the evening the farewell dinner included a speech by Yuan, a speech by the director of tourism in Canton, and two speeches by me. My appreciative pilgrims, after punctuating every tirade with *kampei's*, became roaring drunk. They frantically applauded every sentimental passage, roared with laughter at my least printable jokes, and were shedding a few maudlin tears when the grilled pig was brought in, its head hanging to one side. This great delicacy of Cantonese cuisine had been cut into small pieces and put together again. Encouraged by the Chinese, to whom I had just sworn eternal friendship, I caught a piece of the complicated jigsaw puzzle between my chopsticks. Under the skin all I found was a small square piece of fat. I shut my eyes and swallowed. A gulp of warm wine, and on to the next course. Despite my growing feeling for China I could not warm up to the pig. When it was gone I gratefully breathed in the warm breeze from the River of Pearls.

23

$\mathbf{A}$t dawn the next day we were all ahead of time, hurrying to leave the paradise that was Canton. We settled down on our last Chinese train, two by two and face to face, for a three-hour trip through paddies, hills, and market gardens filled with half-naked peasants, and women in parasol hats. The loud-speaker on the train jabbered shrilly, and I protested.

"There are some people here who want to hear the radio," replied Shin. He was usually friendlier.

There was a muddle over the exit formalities. Shin panicked, and he and the relevant official lost their way among all the orders and counterorders. They ended up asking me for my visa to Hong Kong.

At the frontier we had a very good lunch in a pleasantly cool dining room. I changed my pilgrims' surplus currency and watched the dance of the abacuses with fascination. I had told Yuan that I was worried about customs. Did he think we would be delayed a long time? It would be terribly inconvenient, since our train for Hong Kong left the frontier at one fifteen. Yuan replied that I need not worry: he had warned the customs in advance.

Still, Georges's bag was bulging with old Chinese paintings. Señora Neralinda, the insatiable Peruvian, had had to buy three suitcases in Shanghai to carry her knickknacks. Almost everybody in the party, except Adrienne, who hated "that sort of thing," had bought dozens of Chinese antiques, all marked with the red wax seal that signified that an object could be exported. We walked in single file past two nonchalant, navy-blue customs men—all of us except Boilèle and Mme. Trollan, whom they led into a little side room. I rushed after them. Boilèle, who was being very genial with the Chinese, snarled at me *mezzo voce*, "So this is how you look after our interests! You might at least have spared me this. Fortunately I am the Swedish consul in Lyons, and they can't get away with it."

For the moment, however, they seemed to be getting away with it quite successfully. Three more customs officials, one a middle-aged man who spoke good English, started removing the knickknacks from the general's suitcases one by one, unwrapping them, and lining them up like a row of toy soldiers. Boilèle argued, but for once without shouting. Indeed he was unusually quiet in the presence of the customs men. A quarter of an hour, half an hour went by.

"I'm afraid we may miss our train," I said to Yuan.

Smiling blandly, but with a gleam in his eye that was

180

the nearest thing to malice I had ever seen, Yuan re-assured me. "Don't worry, Madame Modiano, it will soon be over."

At five past one the customs men shut the last of Boilèle's suitcases. The oldest official apologized to me for the delay and said that he was keeping three objects whose wax seals had apparently dropped off. He explained to Boilèle that without their seals these articles could not leave China. It was a flagrant injustice, but I couldn't help finding it funny. The general snarled at the impassive Chinese that thanks to his diplomatic status he expected to receive the confiscated articles in Hong Kong in less than three days. In the corridor leading to the no man's land between the two frontiers, the farther he got from China the more indignant he became. The silence of his companions was almost tangible. Only a minute earlier they had all been joking with our Chinese interpreters about the general. At least Boilèle's tantrums had succeeded in uniting Chinese and Europeans in laughter. And laughing together is a first step to understanding.

As we reached the frontier each of us in turn shook hands with our guides, more or less warmly depending on the European's character and the relations he had had with the Chinese. The Musketeers, Laure, Colette, the Chapeaus, the Blums, and the Adjoufs had a friendly word of thanks for each of the three. Adrienne, Boilèle, and Mme. Trollan made a point of not thanking the Chinese, who bowed and smiled politely all the same. I reflected that Shin, Shu, and Yuan had just spent a whole month satisfying the incomprehensible whims of a bunch of frequently selfish and discourteous capitalists; yet they had become emotionally integrated to some extent with our party. When Isabella shook his hand Shin blushed and looked down. Afterward he followed her with his eyes.

181

When my turn came Yuan squeezed my hands as if he would never stop and said something to me in Chinese. Shin, his eyes bright with tears, was so overcome that he forgot to translate Yuan's words. "I hope that you will show me Paris one day" was all he said.

Dear, grumpy Shu, damp-eyed, stood on tiptoe and did something unknown in China, something she had seen us do among ourselves: she kissed me on both cheeks. With a lump in my throat I picked up my bag and walked away quickly. When I reached the end of the no man's land, I turned around for the last time and saw the three little figures in the distance still waving. I gave a final wave before returning to my own comfortable life. I felt as if I were deserting them, which was illogical, for they were products of a revolution that had given direction to their lives. All three were satisfied with their lot and could not imagine any other, yet they went on waving. They were fond of me, it is true, but possibly they waved also to some vaguely glimpsed freedom, or perhaps simply to the idea of getting out, of "seeing somewhere else," as Shin had said one day.

On the other side of the border there were no more soft caps; there were khaki shorts, black socks, and English accents. In the train a steward offered whisky and cigarettes. Within five minutes it was like a cocktail party. An unrecognizable, smiling Signora Negri went from one compartment to another, toasting the occupants. Chinese women in the stations had bouffant hair styles, tight skirts slit up to the thigh, high-heeled shoes, and a graceful, provocative walk. They were the sisters of the women we had just left, yet nothing was the same. I felt rather sad.

The Mandarin Hotel had the familiar luxuries—a marble bathroom, a panoramic view of one of the most beautiful bays in the world, letters posted in Paris two days before, a hairdresser, a pedicure, and a perky little seven-year-old page who reminded me of Chinese children on the other side except that he expected a tip.

That evening in the noisy bar a few of us sat silently over our glasses of whisky, a little ashamed of all this luxury. We thought of our three Chinese friends waiting in the dingy Canton hotel for the morning train and three days' traveling on hard seats back to Peking and to their life's work, the building of the People's China.

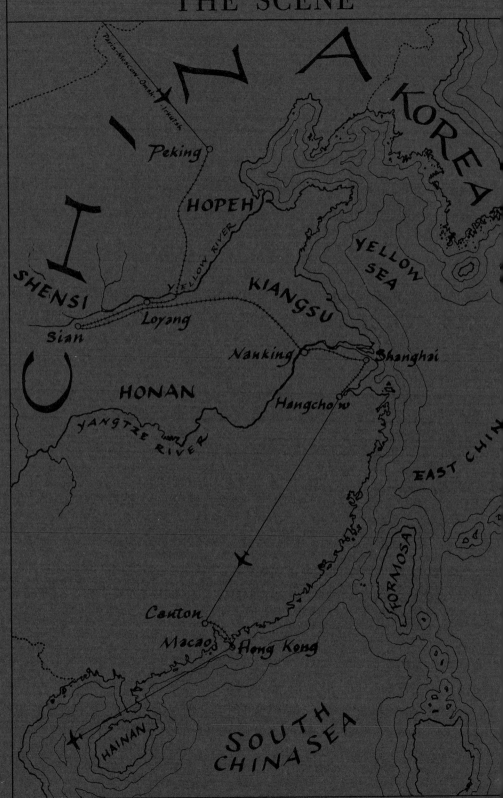

THE SCENE